THE OLD BAILEY AND ITS TRIALS

Main Hall of the Central Criminal Court, looking towards Court No. 2

Photo: Bedford Lemere

THE OLD BAILEY AND ITS TRIALS

By

BERNARD O'DONNELL
Author of "The Trials of Mr. Justice Avory"

The Newgate Knocker

BURKE LONDON

First published 1950
Reprinted 1951
Republished by Burke Publishing Co., Ltd., 1952

Printed in England
for Burke Publishing Co., Ltd.,
55 Britton Street, London, E.C.1.
by
STAPLES PRINTERS LIMITED
at their Rochester, Kent, establishment

CONTENTS

LIST OF ILLUSTRATIONS

ACKNOWLEDGMENT

MANY VOLUMES would be required to deal in any way fully or adequately with the colourful part played by the Old Bailey in the criminal history and the administration of justice in our land. I have therefore tried to give as comprehensive a story of this famous Court as space will allow, together with the outstanding dramas which have been played out within its walls over the centuries.

I express my grateful thanks to Mr A. W. Burt, the Keeper of the Old Bailey, and to Mr Bromley of the Guildhall Library, for the assistance they have given me in compiling this work, and must here make acknowledgment to the various authors whose names are mentioned in the pages which follow.

BERNARD O'DONNELL

January 1950

CHAPTER ONE

THEN AND NOW

IN the dock at the Old Bailey stood five priests charged with high treason. On the Bench of the cramped and sombre court sat the Lord Chief Justice with a dozen others of My Lords the King's Justices. The body of the court was thronged with a restless, murmuring mob, eager for a verdict of "Guilty" against the accused men.

Two of the prisoners protested that they had already been tried on the same charge, and that the evidence was so scant that the previous jury had been dismissed without giving a verdict.

"We say that we ought not to be put in jeopardy of our lives a second time for the same cause," urged one, while the other insisted that "at the former trial we should either have been condemned or acquitted".

There was a pretence of consultation among the judges for a minute or two, and then the Lord Chief Justice spoke.

"It is within the discretion of the court," he declared, "to discharge a jury without taking a verdict where witnesses are wanting, or there is an accident of that nature."

Consider the import of this ruling. It meant that if the prosecution failed to prove its case through producing insufficient evidence, the trial of a prisoner could be adjourned again and again, until a sufficient number of witnesses *could* be obtained.

This was bad enough, yet worse was to come.

The jurors were called, among them being several who had been jurors at the previous trial. Then the evidence was presented. And what evidence! The case against these priests rested almost entirely on the testimony of professional witnesses, paid to swear whatever was required of them.

Their evidence was disproved on a score of points by a score of other witnesses—yet they were held up to the jury by the Lord Chief Justice as witnesses of truth and integrity.

One described how he saw the accused at certain times and at various places in London, and attended their "consults" or secret meetings.

"*When* did you see us, and *where* did you see us," demanded the prisoners, "that we may have an opportunity to show we were in other places."

But again the Lord Chief Justice intervened.

"I perceive that your defence will be little else but captiousness," he said, "to disprove the witnesses in circumstances of place, time, persons and numbers, which are but little matters to the substance."

Here were men on trial for their lives, who could establish alibis, who brought sixteen persons from France to say that the chief witness for the prosecution, who declared he was present at the "consult" in London, had been at St. Omer, in France, on that day. And their defence was described as "captious"!

Later, when permission was asked to call evidence that a prosecution witness had given perjured evidence at the previous trial, the judge refused on the grounds that this would be "trying that cause over again".

"But if he is convicted of perjury in one case, he is not to be believed in another," protested the accused.

The Lord Chief Justice was not to be swayed by any such appeal, and brusquely told the jury that they were not to take any notice of what had transpired in any former trial. And then in his summing-up he concluded:

"The prisoners' defence consists of catching at a point of time; but that is a thing no man can charge his memory with. *You are not to govern your judgments by a mistake of seven or eight days.*"

The year was 1679. The trial was that of five Jesuit priests in connection with what became known as the Popish Plot. They were sentenced to death and, in addition to hanging, suffered the agonising refinement of being drawn and quartered.

Two hundred and sixty-six years later, I sat in Number One Court at the Old Bailey and listened to the trial of William Joyce. The charge was the same—that of high treason. But what a difference in the setting of the trial and in the administration of the law!

In 1945, there was no bench packed with judges determined to secure a verdict of guilty at all costs; instead, a calm, dispassionate judge, Mr Justice Tucker, and one of the finest counsel at the English Bar, Mr G. O. Slade, to make a brilliant defence of the man whose nickname, "Lord Haw-Haw"—invented by my friend Jonah Barrington—will go down in history as a music-hall joke.

And Joyce—what of him? From his voice of braggart pomposity as heard from Bremen over the air, one might have pictured him as a rather dominant figure, both in size and personality. But in the dock he seemed small, with narrow, sloping shoulders; thinning, mouse-coloured hair; cold, calculating eyes that narrowed as they gazed out at judge and jury; a twisted nose, scarred face, and a small thin-lipped mouth.

Such was the man who faced his trial in the September of our year of victory: the victory that he had, with all the eloquence and conviction at his command, tried to make us believe would never be ours.

Only once during that trial was his voice heard. Two words were all that he uttered on his own behalf—"Not Guilty" in answer to the charge read out by the Clerk of the Court. The familiar voice, echoing round the court, was something of a shock. One almost expected to hear the introductory chime which used to herald his broadcasts.

In his closing speech to the jury, Sir Hartley Shawcross, K.C., the Attorney General, said:

"Members of the jury, the onus in this case, as I said to you just now, is firmly fixed upon the Crown, and the last thing the prosecution desires in this case is to exaggerate the facts or to stretch the law. The less you might consider the prisoner entitled to receive justice at the hands of a British Court, the more vitally important is it to see that he secures justice according to law and justice according to the evidence."

There was no ranting denunciation of Joyce or his crime; simply a dispassionate appeal that the jury should apply their common sense in arriving at their verdict.

Remember, too, that the trial of Joyce had been postponed, at the request of the defence, from the July to the September Sessions of the Old Bailey, so that evidence could be obtained from America that Joyce was not a British subject, but a citizen of the United States.

This evidence was of importance, as it left only one count in the indictment, that which charged him with "adhering to the King's enemies elsewhere than in the King's Realm", at a time when he was "a person owing allegiance to our Lord the King". The case for Joyce was that, in view of his American nationality, he owed no allegiance to Britain. But the judge pointed out that, having come to live in England permanently and having "stepped out of this realm" armed with a British passport on the application for which he had described himself as "a British subject by birth", the accused could not shed the allegiance he already owed.

That is precisely what Joyce had done. He had taken every advantage of the hospitality of this country as a self-declared British subject; he had carefully concealed his American nationality from everyone, even on his marriage certificate; he had never sought to claim his rightful nationality until his treachery had rendered his life forfeit. Then, and then only, did he set out to establish his American nationality, and try to prove that Britain had no right to try him because he was an alien. The judge broke down this argument, not by violent diatribe or resort to subterfuge, but by reference to the established law on the point.

Let us take another example of the meticulous care with which Mr Justice Tucker summed-up to the jury. Expounding the law on "aiding and comforting the King's enemies", he stressed that this meant "nothing more than actively throwing in your lot with the enemy, actively assisting the enemy". And to make it perfectly clear that this must be a voluntary act and not one imposed by *force majeure*, he added: "It must be done with the intention of aiding the King's enemies as well."

In conclusion, Mr Justice Tucker made an impressive appeal to the jury, urging them to "be sure that you arrive at what you honestly believe to be a true verdict according to the facts, regardless of opinion or anything of that kind".

The jury were absent only twenty-one minutes before returning with a verdict of Guilty. Joyce stood rigidly to attention during the closing scenes, and when asked whether he had anything to say why sentence of death should not be passed upon him, shook his head sharply. After sentence had been pronounced, he bowed to the judge, turned smartly and walked briskly from the dock.

But the full majesty of British law had not yet been shown. Joyce was allowed to appeal to the Court of Criminal Appeal, where three learned judges including Viscount Caldecott (the then Lord Chief Justice), Mr Justice Humphreys, and Mr Justice Lynskey, sat to hear the legal arguments adduced by his counsel. Joyce was there, a tiny isolated figure in the green baize-covered dock at the side of the court.

The appeal was dismissed.

Joyce apparently still hoped to save his neck. He appealed once more, this time to the House of Lords, the highest tribunal in the land.

A four days' hearing took place before five Law Lords, including the Lord Chancellor. Again the same patient consideration was given to all the arguments for and against the conviction. One judge dissented from the general view, but the others were unanimous that the verdict must stand, and William Joyce died on the scaffold.

I have tried, in describing these contrasting trials, to give a brief glimpse of the Old Bailey over the centuries, for the concern of this book is not only with the changes in the Old Bailey itself, but also with the law administered there. In the pages which follow I shall give other illustrations of how time has brought its changes in the realms of crime and punishment, as recorded in the annals of this the greatest criminal court in the world.

Standing in the very heart of the City of London, at the corner of Newgate Street and the street of Old Bailey, the Central Criminal Court is to-day a fine and stately building. It is surmounted by a copper dome on which stands a bronze statue of Justice, sixteen feet high, looking out over London from a height of two hundred and twelve feet. In her left hand Justice holds the scales which symbolise that the evidence for and against a prisoner on trial in the courts below shall be evenly weighed. Her right hand bears aloft the sword of Justice, a promise of retribution to the convicted wrong-doer.

It is a unique figure, for it is the only statue of Justice in the world which is not blindfolded. When the new building was opened by the late King Edward VII in 1907, the Corporation of London was concerned to impress upon the world that Justice, as administered at the Old Bailey, was not blind. In old Newgate Gaol, which for nearly a thousand years stood upon this same spot, justice had too often meted out cruel punishment and undeserved death.

The Old Bailey! What visions its name conjures up of famous trials; of great figures who have moved across the pages of history towards the dock, and from thence to shameful imprisonment or agonising death.

The Old Bailey! There is almost a lyrical quality about the name. The late Sir W. S. Gilbert, of Gilbert and Sullivan opera fame, made glib use of it in *Trial by Jury*, when he caused his amorously inclined judge to carol:

> "That rich attorney was good as his word,
> The briefs came trooping gaily,
> And every day my voice was heard
> At the Sessions or Ancient Bailey."

The present building, as you will have gathered, is not so ancient in years as in tradition, having been completely rebuilt just over forty years ago. Looking at it to-day in all its dignity and grace of outline—for the Old Bailey's dignity remains, though one corner has suffered damage from a bomb—it is difficult to realise that only some eighty years ago (1868) people were publicly hanged in the street on a spot almost immediately outside the present main entrance. As late as 1833, a boy of nine was sentenced to death in the old Sessions House for stealing twopennyworth of hard paint. The commutation of this youthful felon's sentence to one of being sent to a penitentiary was looked upon as an act of clemency.

Visiting Number One Court to-day and seeing the care with which the interests of a prisoner on trial are safeguarded, one finds it difficult to imagine the conditions of the past. Until 1771, all prisoners, male and female alike, were practically condemned in the eyes of the jury before their trial began, for they were brought to the dock in manacles and leg-irons. Until 1834, all prisoners found guilty on capital charges—there were some two hundred offences carrying the death penalty—were herded together in the dock on the last day of each sessions, to receive the death sentence. Transportation was not abolished in this country till 1853.

Over the portico of the main entrance to the Old Bailey

is a finely sculptured group depicting the Recording Angel supported by the figures of Fortitude and Truth. The Recording Angel must have had a busy time in those not-so-remote days when prisoners were hanged in batches outside the Debtor's Door of Old Newgate, amid the clamour of eager onlookers. The unhappy prisoners who suffered trial there needed all the Fortitude they could summon, to face the punishments inflicted upon them, and there was little veneration for Truth in the evidence given within the walls of the Old Bailey by professional witnesses.

Crowds still throng the Central Criminal Court on the occasion of a sensational murder trial, and people still queue up for hours to gain entrance to the public gallery, but there is greater order among these would-be onlookers than there was a hundred years ago. Until 1860, a fee was charged for entrance to the gallery. These fees were a recognised perquisite of the Keeper of the Court, and the Keeper saw to it that no "House Full" signs were ever displayed outside the gallery entrance.

Just as a trial inside the Old Bailey attracted big crowds, bringing extra money to the Keeper of the Court, so did an execution outside the buildings bring a rich harvest to the owners of nearby houses. The windows of these buildings were let out to those who could afford to pay, in the same way as windows are let out to-day on the route of a Royal Procession. As much as £10 a seat was demanded—worth perhaps five times that sum to-day—and the surrounding viewpoints in the street were thronged with deliriously excited men and women who gathered in position on the eve of the execution, whiling away the long night hours with song and dance and drunken debauch.

Those who had hired rooms overlooking the gallows gave parties at which champagne flowed freely, immorality was rampant, and the writhings on the gallows of the dying prisoners were regarded as an enjoyable addition to the entertainment.

Even high officials of the gaol gave "hanging breakfasts" to their friends and the City officers. One Governor, who gave these feasts regularly, used to have his young daughter to act as hostess for him. The programme on these occasions began with the execution, witnessed from a special place of vantage. Seats were provided, either on the actual gallows, or else on a special platform built nearby. After the execution, the "breakfast" was served in the special dining hall of the prison. It was a splendid feast, held at the Corporation's expense, and therefore garnished with every kind of luxury. More often than not, those present over-primed themselves with wine before they felt fit to savour the next item in this delectable programme—the cutting down of the bodies. Meanwhile, the felons dangled at the ends of their respective ropes, awaiting the pleasure of the Governor and his guests. During this wait they would perhaps be stoned, and pelted with rotten fruit and vegetables, by the surging mob who rioted in the street of Old Bailey, as narrow then as it is to-day.

That some of the onlookers were crushed to death in their sensation-seeking quest, was perhaps a measure of ironic justice. Even as late as 1807 twenty-eight people met such a fate within a few yards of the gallows.

The judges themselves behaved with what we to-day would consider a ghoulish lack of dignity on the occasion of a great trial. They indulged in feasts of gargantuan size. It was the custom for the Lord Mayor and the City Sheriffs to provide a sumptuous meal for distinguished visitors and the higher court officials.

Mr W. Eden Cooper, in his book *History of Newgate and the Old Bailey*, relates how "it was no uncommon thing for judges to return to the bench and pass sentence of death while under the influence of wine, the chaplain or 'ordinary' as he was then called, standing by in the same condition. When persons of distinction visited the court to listen to the death sentence, or view a notorious highwayman, they were invited to partake of the feasts. In 1807-1808 the dinners for three sessions (nineteen days) cost Sheriff Philips £35 per day, the total figures given being £665. During this period 145 dozen of wine were consumed at an additional cost of £450.''

A writer in the *Quarterly Review* of 1836, describing these celebrations, mentions a trial at which the jury could not agree upon their verdict; so the two judges, Mr Justice Park and Mr Baron Garrow, retired to dinner, which ''proceeded merrily; the beefsteaks were renewed again and again and received the solemn sanction of judicial approbation repeatedly. Mr Adolphus told some of his best stories, and the chaplain was on the point of being challenged for a song when the court-keeper appeared with a face of consternation, to announce that the jury, after being very noisy for an hour or so, had sunk into a dull, dead lull, which, to the experienced in such matters, augurs the longest period of consideration which the heads or rather stomachs of the jury can endure.''

The senior judge decided that he would wait till about ten o'clock that night, and if the jury had not returned a verdict by that time, he would have them locked up ''without fire or candle'' until a reasonable hour (about nine) on the Monday morning, which meant that the jury would be locked up without heat or lighting for the whole of Saturday night, Sunday and Sunday night. Fortunately, the jury were able to arrive at a decision by 9 p.m.

You may suppose that the scenes depicted above took place in days long gone by, in medieval times; but I would remind you that these judicial orgies were not abolished till 1877, just over seventy years ago.

The late Montagu Williams, one of the greatest Queen's Counsel of his day, gives in his reminiscences, written in 1890, a graphic description of one of these feasts. He was a guest because he happened to be prosecuting, for the Crown, a man named Hinson who was charged with murder.

''The chaplain-in-ordinary at Newgate'', he writes, ''was a

stout sensual looking man, who seemed as though he were saturated with City feasts. Arrayed in his clerical robes, it was part of his duty, when the solemn sentence of death was pronounced by the judge, to utter the last word 'Amen'. It frequently happened—as it did upon the occasion of the trial of Frederick Hinson—that the jury retired to consider their verdict at about five o'clock or half-past, in the afternoon, which was the hour at which dinners to which I have alluded were given. The judges, counsel, and guests would repair upstairs to these prandial entertainments and would frequently be called down in the middle of their repast for the sentence of death to be passed upon some wretched criminal. When the death-sentence had been passed upon the man Hinson, and, as we were all retracing our steps to the dining-room, the chaplain-in-ordinary turned to me, and in a voice that was broken, but not with emotion, said 'Well, Williams, so you have bagged your bird.' I must confess I was horrified."

Compare these sordid practices with the dignified demeanour of My Lords the King's Justices in recent times.

In the opening of each session at the Old Bailey there is a series of quietly dramatic events from the moment when the clock of Old St Sepulchre's Church across the street chimes the hour of eleven to the entrance of the Lord Mayor in Number One Court, clad in his richest robes of office, wearing the medallion of a thousand glittering gems and carrying his plumed cocked hat. As the first stroke of the clock booms out, the black-robed usher of the court recites his age-old formula:

> "All persons having anything to do before my Lords the King's Justices of Oyer and Terminer and general gaol delivery, for the jurisdiction of the Central Criminal Court, held here this day by adjournment, draw near and give your attendance. God save the King and my Lords, the King's Justices."

As the last words ring out the Lord Mayor enters followed

by his sheriffs, his sword-bearer and the mace-bearer. It is a chapter out of the colourful past, but with none of the old sordid background which I have described.

Those who, unhappily, are brought there to stand their trial can be sure that their cases will receive a careful and patient hearing. They could not have been sure of fair treatment in earlier days, any more than they could have been certain that the punishment meted out to them would not be out of all proportion to the seriousness of their offences.

As late as 1829 prisoners were transported for life for stealing an apron or a piece of bacon, and in one case the King's prerogative of mercy was invoked on behalf of a youth of 17 who had been sentenced to death for stealing.

"His Majesty having been graciously pleased to extend His Royal Mercy unto him on condition of his being transported to the coast of New South Wales . . . for the term of his natural life," is how the formal missive of leniency was worded.

Most certainly I would never have been allowed to go free after having written this book, for the law, and the judges in past ages, gave short shrift to writers and publishers who dared tell the truth about the evil conditions then obtaining. Such writers were imprisoned and, more often than not, their right hands were cut off.

William Camden, the famous antiquarian and one-time headmaster of Westminster School, describes how one named John Stubbs, and his publisher, Page, suffered this penalty for "seditious libel".

Stubbs was a great scholar who had graduated a Cambridge B.A., and had studied law at Lincoln's Inn. An avowed anti-Catholic, he was vigorously opposed to the negotiations then in progress for Queen Elizabeth's marriage to the Catholic Duke of Anjou, and voiced his views in a pamphlet which bore the title: *The Discoverie of a gaping gulf where into England is liable to be plunged by another French marriage if the Lord forbid not the banes by letting her Majestie see not the sin and punishment thereof.*

Writing in the most loyal and loving terms of the Queen, this zealous author raised questions of policy and roundly denounced the Duke. It may have been his suggestion that Elizabeth was likely to be swayed by her French suitor in matters of State which aroused the ire of the Queen, or that she resented his reference to the likelihood that, at her age, she would be unable to bear children.

Whatever it was, she ordered the author's and publisher's hands to be cut off, and both Stubbs and Page had their hands placed on a block, a butcher's cleaver being placed across the wrist joint. A heavy mallet was then brought down upon the cleaver until the hand was severed.

Even that did not quench the fire of Stubb's patriotism.

"I remember, being then present," writes Camden, "that Stubbs, when his right hand was cut off, plucked off his cap with his left hand, and said with a loud voice, 'God save the Queen!' "

I am glad not to have lived in those times. I am sure I would not have acquitted myself as bravely as Stubbs, and I feel, too, that I would have fallen far short of the heroism with which Elizabethan suspects withstood the tortures inflicted to wring from them a confession of their guilt, or to make them conform with the law.

The use of torture to secure a confession ceased in 1640. At least, that is the year of the last recorded instance in England.

But long after that date there was a painful and sometimes fatal practice applied to persuade prisoners to plead to the indictment against them. This was the *Peine Forte et Dure*, more commonly known as pressing to death. The statutory basis of the punishment is to be found in an Act of Edward I, dated 1275, and this Act continued in force until the end of Queen Anne's reign, and probably a little later.

In 1293 a certain bailiff of one of the "hundreds", who had

refused to "put himself upon the inquest" (in other words, plead) in connection with the over hasty hanging of thirteen persons for the murder of some Dutch sailors, was sentenced to prison.

It was ordered that on the day when he ate, he should not drink; that the bread he ate should be of the worst quality, and the drink be putrid, and that he should be naked in his cell except for a linen garment. In addition he was to lie upon the naked ground, and be loaded with iron from the hands to the elbow and from the feet to the knees, until he should make his submission.

Later, refinements were added to this means of persuasion. A special room called the Press Room was set up beneath the Old Bailey for carrying out *Peine Forte et Dure*. Here, prisoners were spreadeagled upon the stone-flagged floor, their arms and legs tautly outstretched and secured. Heavy weights were then put upon their bodies until their ribs cracked, their breath was crushed out of them—or they pleaded to the charge on which they were being held.

Major Strangeways, charged in February 1658 with the murder of his brother-in-law, refused to plead. Lord Chief Justice Glynn, who presided at the Old Bailey that session, ordered: "That he be put into a mean house (the Press Room) stopped from any light, and be laid upon his back with his body bare; That his arms be stretched forth with a cord the one to one side, the other to the other side of the prison, and in like manner his legs be used; and that upon his body be laid as much iron and stone as he can bare and more. The first day he shall have three morsels of barley bread, and the next he shall drink thrice of the water in the next channel to the prison door, but of no spring or fountain water, and this shall be his punishment till he die."

Clad in white, and covered with a cloak of deep black, Strangeways was taken to the Press Room and a door was placed over him upon which were placed heavy iron weights together with some stones. "He was prohibited that usuall Favour in that kind, to have a sharp piece of Timber layed under his Back to Accellerate its penetration," the record states.

Sturdy of build and strong, he was able to withstand the test, and endured the agony without murmur, but his friends, who had obtained permission to be with him during this ordeal, decided to hasten his end, and stood on him.

In the Thomasson Tracts in the British Museum, there is the following description of this gesture of comradeship:

"The assistants laid on at first Weight, which, finding too light for a sudden Execution, many of those standing by, added their burthens to disburthen him of his pain . . . In the space of eight or ten minutes at most, his unfettered Soul left her tortured Mansion, And he from that violent Paroxisme falls into the quiet sleep of Death."

Pressing to death for refusing to plead was abandoned some time during the early 18th century, but it was not until 1827 that it became law to enter a plea of Not Guilty against a prisoner who "stood mute", as it was called. Until 1772, in the reign of George III, all "mutes" were found Guilty and sentenced, as if they had been convicted by a jury.

And "persuasion" was used on other persons than prisoners. Recalcitrant juries who disagreed, or took a longer time to return a verdict than the judges thought fit, were carried around the City in a cart so that a jeering populace could express their contempt for men so heedless of their duties as citizens.

Under the Tudors and Stuarts it was the custom to make jurors answer for their verdict before the King's Council, and at one time they were liable to fine or imprisonment by the Star Chamber. Even after the abolition of the Star Chamber the Crown made use of the judges to intimidate juries.

Bribery of juries, if not exactly rife, was at least existent. In addition the law did not always ensure that there was no contact between a juror and a material witness in a case, whereas to-day, of course, such contact is forbidden.

The bribing of hangmen to ensure quick despatch was also common practice, but one can understand this in view of the prolonged nature of an execution in bygone days. The more fortunate, who were wealthy enough to be able to afford a substantial bribe to be "turned off" quickly, or whose friends were prepared to tip the hangman if he did a swift job of work, always received the best attention.

"Turning off quickly" had reference to the manner in which a condemned prisoner was forced to mount a ladder to the gallows, the ladder being "turned" and the prisoner thus left dangling at the end of his rope. Sometimes the prisoner swung there for fifteen or twenty minutes, alive, half conscious, his body twitching grotesquely to the amusement of onlookers and the anguish of friends. Sometimes these friends would mount the gallows, and cling to the suspended body, pulling and jerking in the hope of hastening the end.

Perhaps there is an ironic satisfaction in the knowledge that not a few of the hangmen with whom we shall make acquaintance in later chapters met their death on the same gallows on which they had so brazenly strutted and performed but a few years before; and also in the knowledge that a sprinkling of judges who had passed sentence of death upon prisoners came to a similar untimely end.

But enough of these horrors for the time being. It is clear that many of the brutalities and injustices that stained the administration of our laws in London existed until comparatively recent times. But let us leave consideration of crime, prison, and the law past and present, and try to trace the origin of the Old Bailey as it was in the beginning.

CHAPTER TWO

NEWGATE AND THE SOCIAL SCENE

IF one stands on the corner of the street of Old Bailey, looking towards Holborn, and watching the busy crowds and unceasing streams of traffic passing to and fro, it is difficult to conjure up a picture of London as a walled city, to which entrance could only be obtained through one or other of its various gates. But so it was a thousand years ago; and relics of the Roman wall which surrounded the old city remain to this day.

When excavations were being made on the site of the present Old Bailey, evidence was found that this ancient wall ran along the east side of where the court now stands. Remains of an old Roman gateway and a surrounding moat were also discovered.

This gate, which was called Newgate, was not only the main western approach to medieval London, it was also the place where, for centuries, felons and malefactors, debtors and trespassers were held while awaiting trial, and kept prisoner after they had been convicted.

This was the beginning of Newgate Gaol. It was also the scene of some of the earliest trials in former times, and may well be regarded as the birthplace of what we now know as the Old Bailey.

As we stand on this historic corner, then, let us try to visualise that London of the past. First, picture a steep hill running down from Newgate, past the spot where Holborn Viaduct Station now stands, to the River Fleet. One can see no trace of this river to-day, for it is a bricked over sewer running underground from Hampstead to the River Thames near Blackfriars. Yet, round about the year 1300, the Fleet was "of such width and depth that ten or twelve naves (ships) were wont to come to Flete Bridge, and some of them to Holebourne Bridge".

Farringdon Street now runs over part of the covered in River Fleet, and the ornate Viaduct, near to the City Temple, now marks the site of the old Holebourne Bridge.

Having obtained this brief glimpse of London as a walled in city, and more particularly of the immediate vicinity around Newgate, let us try to lift the curtain of time on the history of the old gaol, and of the Old Bailey in its earliest days as a criminal court. The story of the Old Bailey is inseparable from that of Newgate. The histories of both are so interwoven that it is impossible to relate the one without including the other. What little we know of this early history is so absorbing and colourful that it is a pity the records are so few.

Writers throughout the ages have referred to Newgate either by name or inference. The earliest mention is probably that by William Fitzstephen, clerk to Thomas à Becket, in his history of the London of that time:

"On the west are two towers very strongly fortified with the great high wall of the City, having seven double gates."

That was written some years before Fitzstephen died in 1190; and while there is no specific mention of Newgate, there is no doubt that New Gate—as it would then be called—was one of the seven double gates of the City, and was in fact the gate to the west with its two strongly fortified towers. It is equally certain that, by this time, Newgate was being used as a prison as well as a gateway to the City. In the records of King John (1199-1216), mention is made of Newgate as a place for "keeping felons and tresspassers".

In a Pipe Roll of 1188, in the reign of Henry II, there is mention of a sum of 66 shillings and 8 pence to be paid for land on which the gaol was to be built, and in a later Pipe Roll of 1190 the gaol is mentioned as Newgate.

That the gaol was embodied in the gate is in accordance with the customs of the times. Every city gate had its keep, for holding or "keeping" an offender.

There is evidence that there was a gate at this same spot centuries before it became known as Newgate. Most antiquarians agree that the site of Newgate was also the site of the West Gate of Saxon London. In a charter of Burhred of Mercia dated 857, it is mentioned as "Westgetum". Later on we hear of it as Chamberlain's Gate, the old gate and wall having long fallen into ruin. From Domesday Book one learns that William the Chamberlain paid 6 shillings a year for his vineyard at Holborn, which indicates that in 1086 the Chamberlain had property outside the City gate.

The Chamberlain was originally the City Treasurer and a King's officer. In the City he had his own court in which he heard and gave judgment in disputes between masters and apprentices. What more likely, then, that this gate should be known as Chamberlain's Gate because that officer had his court there? And what more likely that when this gate fell into ruins, making necessary the building of a new gate, the new structure should be named New Gate?

John Stow in his monumental *Survey of London and Westminster* (1598) has his own idea as to how the name originated. He says:

"This gate (Newgate) was first erected about the reign of Henry I or King Stephen, upon this occasion: the cathedral church of St Paul being burnt about the year of 1086 in the reign of William the Conqueror, Mauritius, then Bishop of London repaired not the old church, as some have supposed, but began a new work such as men then judged would never have been performed . . . After Mauritius, Richard Beamore did wonderfully advance the work of the said church, purchasing the large streets and lanes round about, wherein were wont to dwell many lay people, which grounds he began to compass about with a strong wall of stone and gates."

So that within the high outer wall of London, there was this other wall surrounding the new church, about which Stow continues:

"By means of this increase of church territory, but more by enclosing ground for so large a cemetery or churchyard, the high and large street stretching from Aldgate in the east until Ludgate in the west, was in this place so crossed and stopped up that the carriage through the city westward was forced to pass without the said churchyard wall on the north side through Paternoster Row; and then south down Ave Mary Lane, and again west through Bowyer Row to Ludgate . . . which passage by reason of so often turning was very cumbersome and dangerous, both for horse and man; for remedy whereof a *new gate* was made and so called, by which men and cattle with all manner of carriages might pass more directly (as afore) from Aldgate through West Cheap by Paul's on the north side; through St Nicholas Shambles and Newgate market to Newgate, and from thence to any part westward over Oldbourne Bridge, or turning without the gate into Smithfield and through Isledon (Islington) to any part north and by west."

According to Stow it appears that the New Gate was built because the knights, merchants and pilgrims coming up from Canterbury towards Middle England, found their way through Ludgate blocked by the dumps of building materials for old St Paul's, then in course of erection. So the new gate was rebuilt at the northern end of the street of Old Bailey where the city wall turned sharply.

Stow goes on to say that "This gate hath of long time been a gaol or prison where felons and tresspassers, as appeareth by records in the reign of King John and of other kings . . ."

In the annals of the City Corporation one can find reference to the committal of prisoners to Newgate from the year 1218, and in the reign of Henry III (1216-1272), the King wrote to the Sheriffs of London, ordering them to repair Newgate, with a promise that the cost would be borne by the Exchequer of that day.

The Sheriffs of London and Middlesex were responsible for the safe keeping of prisoners, the Keeper or Gaoler being their deputed official.

In 1241 some rich Jews, whose criminal exploits were purely imaginary, were ordered to pay 20,000 marks, or be kept perpetual prisoners at Newgate and other prisons.

During this same year it is recorded that Henry sent certain sheriffs to the Tower, and fined the City 3,000 marks for allowing a convicted priest to escape from Newgate. As Stow puts it:

"And the same king fined them (the citizens of London) at 3,000 marks for the escape of a prisoner out of Newgate of whom they took no charge; for he was a Clarke, prisoner to the Bishop of London, under the custody of his own servants, and as for the place, it was onely borrowed of the Londoners to serve that turne."

So there is ample evidence as to the antiquity of Newgate as a prison.

It is interesting to speculate how the name Old Bailey first came to be given to that narrow little street running from Ludgate Hill to the corner of Newgate Street, and how it eventually came to be applied to the court or Sessions House which was eventually built in that street.

Several explanations have been put forward at different times. Stow suggests that the street of Old Bailey was derived from the *Ballium*, or outer space beyond the City Wall. Maitland, on the other hand, refers to it as Bail Hill, a high place where the bail or sheriff lived and held his court.

A bailey was an open space enclosed by fortifications and sometimes these were known as "wards". If there was more than one line of fortification they would be known as the inner and outer baileys. Thus the Old Bailey may have been situated in one of the baileys which were part of the old City fortifications, and may have come by its name from this fact.

As I have indicated, the records are scanty, and opinions vary as to the earliest origins of both Newgate Gaol and the Old Bailey. We only know that in Roman times, when London was a walled city, there was a gate giving access to the City on the site where the Old Bailey now stands. We know that from earliest times this gate was used as a prison, which gained notoriety as an evil, pestiferous place where the laws of the country were administered with almost bestial cruelty. That prison was known as Newgate.

Before there was any courthouse, before there was anything approaching the majesty of justice as we know it to-day, prisoners were tried in the gaol itself. Thus we have another link connecting Newgate with Old Bailey, for in ancient times Newgate was both a place of trial and a prison.

It is interesting to note that one of the first recorded trials to take place in the Old Bailey, in 1334, was of a man who would to-day be described as a cat burglar. He was one John de Sloghtre, who called himself a chaplain. He was arrested in the very act of climbing into the top window of a City goldsmith, and when captured was found to be carrying several daggers in his pockets.

For this unclerical offence he was first put into the Tun, a small prison in Cornhill, "for being found wandering", as Riley's *Memorials of London* puts it. "Afterwards on the Saturday following, he was taken before the Mayor, and because he was carrying arms against the peace and against the cry (hue and cry) before made in the City, he was committed to the Gaol of Newgate."

We have no direct knowledge of whether de Sloghtre was tried in the gate-house prison, or whether the court was held in one of the special buildings in the Old Bailey, hired for the occasion. But that is rather leaping ahead of our story. Long before that record there were other trials in what was the very early equivalent of the Old Bailey. First came those terrible hush-hush trials in Newgate Gaol itself, the hapless prisoner being held for some months, perhaps, before he was brought to trial.

There were no newspapers in those days to call attention to a miscarriage of justice. The so-called "Sessions" were held only once a year, if they were held at all, so that a prisoner might lie in this fetid, fever-ridden gaol for almost any length of time, a victim of brutality and suffering, and with the knowledge that, as like as not, death would be the punishment meted out to him.

Later, trials were held in special rooms, or "covered places", outside the precincts of the prison. These rooms were hired by the Sheriffs and paid for by the City Corporation.

Apart from the trials conducted in these places, the main concern of the Sheriffs and Aldermen was to make sure that His Majesty's judges were handsomely entertained to the feast which I have already described in the first chapter.

Records of Newgate Gaol for the 13th and 14th centuries are very scarce. We know that in 1256 several men were committed to Newgate for using "kidels" and illegal nets. These were fixed nets at points of the Thames to prevent free usage of the river. In 1298 Sir Hugh Despenser, Forest Justiciar for this side of the Trent, ordered that one Saer le Barber should "be attached by his body and sent to Newgate in order that he might appear before me to answer for the trespass", the trespass being that the said Saer had (among other things) declared Sir Hugh to be "unworthy of praise".

We know that such was the condition of the prison and so grievous was the state of the prisoners that in 1337 Sir J. Poultney gave "four marks by the year to the relief of the prisoners in Newgate". It was so overcrowded, and its sanitation so primitive, that Thomas Knoles, grocer and sometime Mayor of London, "caused sweet water to be conveyed to the gates of Newgate and Ludgate for reliefe of the prisoners there". In 1385 Sir William Walworth "gave somewhat to relieve the prisoners in Newgate, so have many others since," declares Stow.

We can appreciate how necessary these gifts were, when we know something of the conditions which prevailed for centuries in spite of everything that the reformers of those days could do. Convicts serving their sentences were mixed indiscriminately with men, women and children awaiting trial. At that time, when Sessions were held only once a year, people of both sexes, young and old alike, spent months in the degrading and demoralising atmosphere of the prison before they were brought before the King's justices.

The keepers, or gaolers, were openly permitted to charge fees to prisoners for privileges such as better food and accommodation. Even the Governor of the prison was able to add to his income by allowing unlimited drinking in his gaol, the profits from the sale of drink being one of his perquisites. In the time of Queen Elizabeth, the office of warden was granted as a valuable bequest or perquisite to be held through life. Fees for safe custody were levied upon prisoners and were exacted by all forms of cruelty.

In the course of time it became the custom to sell the reversion of this popular office. It is recorded that £3,000 was paid for a keeper's job in Newgate. A Captain Richardson bartered his lucrative position for this sum. One John Huggins was charged an even larger amount by Lord Clarendon, who demanded £5,000 in return for making Huggins Keeper at Fleet. In the fourteenth century the King occasionally brought pressure to bear to get the Keeper's office for one of his dependants.

One can imagine the conditions which must have existed in Newgate Gaol when such bribery and corruption were rife. The young and innocent of both sexes were in daily contact with the most vicious and depraved; the men and women prisoners, sentenced for life and lost to all sense of decency or shame, gave way to indescribable orgies of lust and depravity.

As Major Griffiths says in his *Chronicles of Newgate*,

The door at Newgate through which came condemned persons to their execution

From an etching by Sir D. Y. Cameron, R.A.

"Drunkenness, gaming, profligacy of the vilest sort went forward in the prison without let or hindrance."

Children were born in this cesspool of vice, and, if one died, the stinking rags were torn from its body to cover another yet living. A condemned woman would be haled off to the gallows with perhaps a child at her breast and two or three others clinging to her skirt.

The Keeper would charge a fee for supplying water. There are records of the Court of Aldermen forbidding this practice, but it went on just the same. Prisoners were manacled night and day—unless they could afford to pay the regular fee to the Keeper to have their irons struck off. Prisoners acquitted in open court were dragged back into prison because they were unable to pay the Keeper's illegal fees. All sorts of levies were made by the officers of the prison from the Keeper down to the lowest hireling. Even the prisoners themselves imposed a charge for what they called "chummage" upon newcomers. This entitled the "new boy" to get near the fire, and protected him from the persecution of other prisoners.

Then there was the "cellarman", one of the privileged prisoners—most likely a toady of the Keeper—who was allowed to sell candles at his own price. And woe betide the prisoner who, awaiting his trial or serving his first sentence, did not take advantage of these opportunities to hand over as much money as he could to his more experienced ward-mates. Refusal probably meant being stripped and beaten.

Can you picture the scenes which went on under such circumstances? Lunatics raved up and down the wards, the butt of the callous wretches who had no pity for these human derelicts. Prostitutes were admitted to ply their trade on payment of a shilling. Men and women condemned to be hanged mixed freely with the other prisoners, carousing wildly in the face of imminent death; and, with drunken bravado, shouting aloud the dying speeches they would make on the scaffold, which seems to have been the last thought of many of them.

Some of these speeches attained quite a lyrical note.

There was a more profligate side to old Newgate Gaol, known as the Press Yard or Castle, where felons and prisoners of State who were rich enough to pay for more luxurious accommodation could be provided with all the comfort they desired, by financial arrangement with the Head Keeper of the prison.

The Keeper would charge a premium for the favour of taking over the new lodgement with its fittings, and the figure might range from any reasonable sum to as much as £500. In the Castle the highly favoured were able to indulge their various whims and vices almost without restriction. They could entertain their women, have them to share their luxurious "cells", and entertain their other friends. At a price, arranged with the Keeper, prostitutes were admitted to this part of the gaol, and marriages—some of them mock marriages—were carried out.

Major John Bernhardi, for example, who was imprisoned in Newgate for forty years without trial, was married in Newgate to a woman who bore him ten children. He died in the prison in his eighty-second year.

Nor were the horrors I have described a picture of conditions many centuries past. A Mr Newman, Keeper of the gaol in 1817, giving evidence before a Committee enquiring into conditions at the prison, admitted that he let rooms in his private apartments to wealthy prisoners. He received as much as thirty guineas a week for a single room.

Small wonder that the inhabitants of this unsavoury world of crime became debased in mind and morals, no matter what fine qualities they may have possessed before they entered Newgate. A few, as we shall see, managed to survive this demoralising squalor and succeeded in rising above their surroundings. But the majority, particularly in the Common side of the gaol, sank lower and lower until they became eager to take part in the most bestial scenes.

In 1406 the Common Serjeant, John Westone, had lodged a complaint before the Committee of the Common Council, protesting that women prisoners had to pass through a part of the prison where male prisoners were held. He asked the right to build a tower on the site of the house next door to Newgate Gaol, and having secured permission, he made this building into a women's prison, which remained there until 1422 when, according to Stow, "Licence was granted to John Coventry, Jenkin Carpenter and William Grove, executors to Richard Whittington, to re-edify the jaol of Newgate, which they did with his goods."

Richard Whittington was, of course, none other than the famous Dick of pantomine fame, who was "thrice Lord Mayor of London" and as popular among the people as his famous cat.

It was a strange monument for his executors to raise to his memory, this new edition of Newgate Gaol. In after years the prison became known as "Whittington's Palace". Later, in Cromwellian times, it became known as "The Signe of the Death's Head in the Old Bailie", and is so described in a historical document of that period.

Details of the Whittington building are few, but we have one brief item of extreme value in the form of a sketch drawn by a one-time prisoner of Newgate. The sketch is the frontispiece of a book written by Thomas Bayly, which bears the somewhat lengthy title of *Herba Parietis, or the Wall Flower as it grew out of the Stone Chamber belonging to the Metropolitan Prison of London called Newgate*. It is the first known picture of Newgate, showing the towers on either side of a fine arched gateway, with wall-flowers growing over its upper windows.

During the excavations which were carried out in 1904 to lay the foundations of the present Old Bailey, the only trace found of Whittington's prison was the remains of the water-course which had been laid down by that kindly soul, Thomas Knoles, which "conveyed the waste of water at the cistern near to the common fountain and chapel of St. Nicholas, to the jaols of Newgate and Ludgate for the relief of the prisoners''.

However good the intentions of Dick Whittington may have been, it must be regretfully confessed that his new building brought little improvement in conditions to the prisoners, as we shall see. His prison existed until 1770, when the last Newgate Gaol was begun, a healthier and larger gaol, yet one beset by many of the old evils.

In the meantime, there had been developments in other directions. Instead of trials taking place only once or perhaps twice a year, Sessions were held three and even four times a year. It thus became harder for the Sheriffs to procure a suitable building or ''covered place'' in which the trials could be held.

Then, as the years went by, the City became more and more crowded with merchants, the lanes and squares around Newgate became occupied by the well-to-do, and accommodation for dispensing law was more and more difficult to find. So in 1539 the City officials determined to have their own Justice House.

The subsequent Sessions House was in fact the first Old Bailey in the real sense of the term. It was the first time that any specific court had been used for the trial of prisoners delivered from Newgate, and hence a great step in the evolution of the administration of justice had been taken. It came about in the form of a resolution passed by the Court of Aldermen, and in a further resolution passed in the same year by the Court of Common Council.

The necessity for the building of a Sessions House is indicated in the opening paragraph of that resolution, which I give in its archaic form of expression:

''Forasmoche as comonly prisons where Theeffes and other malefactors be detigned for their offenses be many times vysyted with syknes and by reason thereof the place ys infectyd and moche peryll and daungyer hath chauncyd to the Justyces and other worshipful cominers attendying upon the Justyces for delyveraunce of the Kynges gaole; And forasmoche as there ys no conveyent place wtyn this cytye for that purpose where the sayd delyverie shalbe made; And thys Cytye and Shryeffes of London for the tyme beying be greatly burdened for a conveyent place to be hyred yerely for the same; It is nowe agreed for the comfort of all thys Cytye that a conveyent place be made for that purpose holsomly to be orderyd and prepared upon the common grownde of thys Cytye yn the olde bayly of London wt all spede at the charged of the Chmbre of London."

In 1419, gaolers and prisoners alike, to the number of sixty-four, died from the fever which raged through the prison. This, and the need to provide a suitable place for "feasting" as well as for trying the prisoners, was the main inspiration for building the Justice (or Sessions) House in 1550 upon a spot on the same side of the road as Newgate Gaol and next door to that unhappy building.

The new building was less sinister in appearance than its neighbour, but not much less sinister in applying the law of the land to those who found their way there. Nor did the fact that it was nicely surrounded with gardens, for the "easement" of the Lord Mayor and the King's Justices, lessen the barbarity wreaked upon the prisoners.

But, having built their Sessions House, the City Corporation felt that, as it had cost them so much and was only used on comparatively rare occasions, it should be let to an "honest freeman" of the City at a reasonable rental.

The new Sessions House suffered in the Great Fire of London in 1666. It was not destroyed, but it required a great deal of repair work and partial rebuilding. Naturally in the process some improvements were carried out, notably the inclusion of a fine dining-room over the court, for "feasting". But for the time being let us leave the history of Newgate and the Old Bailey, having gleaned some idea of their joint development through the ages, and turn to some of the earliest trials.

CHAPTER THREE

EARLIEST TRIALS

IN 1327 Edward III granted concession that the Lord Mayor of London should be one of the Justices for gaol delivery of Newgate, and ordered that he should be named in every Commission for that purpose. We know that trials took place in the prison itself, or in special premises hired for the purpose until the erection of the Justice House in 1550, but the records of those early trials are very sparse.

Until the execution of Wille Wawe in 1417, only those hearings which attained the importance of what are called the State Trials, were thought worth reporting by the chroniclers of that day. The ordinary criminal gained no publicity. Even Wille Wawe only attained a brief mention to the effect that in "that same yere (1417) a theffe was i-callyd Wille Wawe was hangyd at Tyborne".

Then there was John de Hakford, charged in 1364 with conspiracy against the chief men of the city. He was sentenced to imprisonment for a year and a day, it being further ordered that "the said John within such year shall four times have the punishment of the pillory; that is to say, one day in each quarter of the year . . . and in this manner.

"The said John shall come out of Newgate without hood or girdle, barefoot and unshod, with a whetstone hung by a chain from his neck and lying on his breast, it being marked with 'A false liar'; and there shall be a pair of trumpets trumpeting before him on his way to the pillory; and there the cause of his punishment shall be solemnly proclaimed."

It is not until we come to the 16th century that we have a more or less continuous record of the savage punishments meted out with lavish hand to wrongdoers. Nearly every form of theft carried the death penalty. If a man dared to suggest that a person holding an official post had been guilty of some judicial error or of speaking other than the truth, he was punished with the pillory or the whipping post, and possibly branded with a hot iron for good measure.

Sir Thomas More, writing of the reign of Henry VIII, remarked that "there might be seen twenty thieves hanging on a single gibbet". On every high road throughout the country a gallows was to be seen, and in many places they were used as signposts.

In 1535, Sir Thomas More was himself beheaded on a charge of high treason. He had "stubbornly opposed the King's second marriage" and refused to recognise King Henry VIII as head of the church. The fact that he had been elected to the House of Commons, where he was chosen as Speaker, had been Treasurer to the Exchequer, and succeeded Wolsey as Lord Chancellor, availed him nothing. More had "maliciously refused to declare his opinion of the Act of Supremacy", and was convicted of treason.

In Salmon's *Critical Review of the State Trials* the writer comments on More's trial: "The jury were so managed that within a quarter of an hour after they were gone out, returned with their Verdict that the Prisoner was guilty."

Later on, Salmon declares: "Very precarious was the life of a subject in this reign. Whatever the court were pleased to denominate treason, was adjudged treason; no jury or Court of Justice durst refuse to convict any man the King intimated he would have condemned to death; and Parliaments met only to execute the King's Decrees."

How very true was this condemnation. It is estimated that during the reign of Henry VIII no fewer than 72,000 of his subjects were executed up and down the country.

As for the refinements of cruelty in Henry's reign, it is only necessary to recall that in 1530 began the practice of boiling convicted poisoners to death. This mode of punishment was begun when one Richard Roose or Coke "of his moste wyked and damnable dysposicyon dyd caste a certeyne venym or poyson into a vessell replenysshed with yeste or barme stondying in the Kechyn of the Reverende Father in God John Bysshopp of Rochester at his place in Lamehyth Marsshe", otherwise Lambeth Palace.

Some porridge or gruel being made in the vessel and fed to the bishop's household, sixteen of the latter died, with the result that poisoning was made an offence of high treason. Fortunately the "bishop himselfe hee eate no pottage that day whereby hee escaped".

Nor was Roose the only victim of this barbarous punishment, for in 1542 Margaret Davy, a maid-servant, suffered a similar fate for poisoning the members of three households in which she had lived.

Henry VIII, as fickle in his religion as in his love, kept the gallows at Tyburn busy and the fires of Smithfield continually ablaze with the victims of his religious persecution. In 1533 he had no fewer than 27 "heretics" burnt to death, among them the Bishop of Rochester who had escaped death at the hands of Roose.

It is some gleam of ironic relief among all this butchery to learn that about this time one or two hangmen found their way to the gallows, there to perish in the same manner as so many of their victims. In 1538 a gentleman by the name of Cratwell, described as "hangman of London", made his appearance as the central figure of a hanging drama in company with two other persons. Cratwell was notorious for the callous manner in which he carried out his duty, and, although the public had not failed to acclaim his prowess in providing them with good entertainment on previous occasions, thousands of people turned up to watch his own debut as victim.

"And the Sonday after Bartelmew day," the records say, "was one Cratwell hangman of London and two persones hanged at the wrestlyng place on the backesyde of Clerkenwell besyde London, for robbing a bouthe in Bartholomew fayre, at which execution was aboue twentie thousand people as I myself judged.'' There is no mention of how he comported himself upon the gallows nor the sort of reception he got from his audience.

Cratwell was probably tried at one of the hired session houses, for the new Justice Hall was not built then, but in 1556 a one-legged hangman stumped his way into the dock of the Justice House on a charge of theft. Unfortunately there is no record of the name of this man, and the only knowledge we have of him is that contained in Machyn's Diary, which relates that on ''the ij day of July rod in a care (cart) v (five) unto Tyborne: on was the hangman with the stump-lege for theft, whyche he had hanged mony a man and quartered mony, and hed (beheaded) mony a nobull man and odur (other)''.

As an instance of how long prisoners were occasionally kept awaiting trial, the case of Thomas Empson in 1540 is of interest. Empson was a monk of Westminster and his offence was that he denied the supremacy of Henry VIII, and refused to ask the King's pardon for so doing; nor would he be sworn to the King's claim to be supreme head of the church. His monk's habit was torn from his body, and he was flung into Newgate. There he remained for over three years, herded in with every type of offender from thieves and footpads to beggars and murderers, many awaiting trial, and others awaiting execution. At the end of that time he was ''brought before the Justices of goale deliverie at Newgate'' on 4 August, 1540, and —that is all we know. No further details either as to his trial or sentence are forthcoming. It is generally believed that he suffered hanging at Tyburn in company with others on that same day, all of them having been ''attainted by parliament for deniall of the King's supremacie''.

Empson's three years is by no means a record, for in the 17th century Thomas Coo remained for a much longer time in Newgate without trial.

I have been unable to trace the charge on which Coo was committed to Newgate, but some time in 1618 he appealed to Sir Julius Caesar and Sir Fulk Greville, complaining that his unmasking of the London insurrection, as a result of which the life of the King had been saved, had only brought "famine and a dungeon" as a reward.

No notice was taken of this appeal, however, and *fifteen years later* he sent his lame child with a letter in which he made a "submission from Newgate dungeon dunghill almost famished", declaring his "contrition of heart" and saying that he was ready to undergo any penance if only the reason for his punishment were made known to him. His long imprisonment had "stripped him even of the clothes on his back", said the letter.

Again there was no response, and another six years passed by. Then he once more petitioned the Council. I cannot trace any result of this petition, and I do not know the fate of poor Coo.

The interval between arrest and trial was not always so great, as witness the instance of a woman named Housden, who, in 1712, was charged with coining, an offence punishable with death. During her trial at the Old Bailey her paramour, a professional highwayman named Johnson, appeared in court and asked permission of the principal warden—called "turnkey" in those days—to speak to the woman in the dock. Mr Spurling, the warder, explained that the trial was in progress, and that no interruption could possibly be allowed, whereupon Johnson pulled out his gun and shot Spurling dead, the virago in the dock loudly applauding the chivalry of her lover.

As soon as the Recorder of the City of London, who was trying the case, recovered from his surprise, he stopped the proceedings, sent the woman prisoner below, and had an immediate indictment made out charging Johnson with murder. He then had Johnson and Housden put in the dock together, the one charged with murder, the other with being an accessory before and after the act. Each received sentence of death.

So Johnson was arrested, tried and sentenced within an hour of having committed the crime.

The alien question, and the extreme care with which governments of to-day keep a close check on foreigners entering the country, is by no means new. Henry VIII sponsored an Act in 1540 driving out all aliens not furnished with "letters of denization". The grounds for the introduction of this Act was that the advent of these strangers in such large numbers was to the "detriment, hindrance, loss and impoverishment of the subjects of his realm", and "to the great decay of the same".

Once more the "wide boys" got busy, just as they do in these days to circumvent any new law. Ralph Egerton, who was in the employ of the then Lord Chancellor, Lord Audley, and thus perfectly placed to work what we now call the passport racket, secured the King's great seal, which he promptly began to impose on a number of documents written out by a confederate named Thomas Harman.

Unfortunately for this enterprising pair, their scheme came to light, and Egerton was hanged, drawn and quartered. Harman's fate is unknown.

His fate, however, was no deterrent to one named Penedo, who in 1570 was convicted at the Justice or Sessions House of counterfeiting the seal of the Queen's Bench Court for an improper purpose. He was luckier than Egerton, however, for he was not sentenced to death. Or was he so lucky after all? He was ordered to be put in the pillory, with one ear nailed to the side in such a position that he would tear it away when he moved. On the second day, his other ear was to be served in the same way.

News of a similar, but more complicated, case of forgery comes to hand as I write. Idel Weingarten, a 46-years old Pole, was sentenced in 1948 at the Old Bailey for what was described as one of the most audacious passport rackets ever to be investigated by Scotland Yard's Special Branch.

Weingarten worked in collaboration with two temporary examiners at the Passport Office. Two other men obtained the use of identity cards and birth certificates from people who were willing, in return for £1, to loan them for a few days. Meanwhile the Pole made his way to a camp for displaced persons near Frankfort, Germany, to obtain photographs of persons who wanted British passports. With these, Weingarten returned to England, where he visited the Passport Office, taking with him the aliens' photographs and the borrowed birth certificates and identity cards. The two temporary examiners supplied the passports, and Weingarten took them to the camp in Germany. Armed with British passports the aliens were able to enter England without trouble.

It was a very lucrative ruse, for in one instance Weingarten received two diamond bracelets worth £500 and a gold watch for his trouble; in another instance he was paid £200; one man gave him gold articles and a camera worth between £300 and £400. At his trial he admitted having obtained at least 26 forged passports. Detective Inspector George Smith, giving evidence of the prisoner's character, told the court that before bringing one alien through the customs at Dover, Weingarten filled the man's pockets with jewellery and notes. He was neither hanged, drawn, quartered nor sent to the pillory. His sentence was two years' imprisonment, a remarkable change from the brutality which was rife in the Elizabethan era.

In the year 1583, at the sessions "holden at Newgate", eleven men were condemned to death for the theft of one horse. They were hanged at Smithfield on a Friday, the day on which horses were brought to the market, in the hope, no doubt, that such a spectacle would have a salutary effect upon would-be horse thieves.

One cannot pass from this age without reference to a trial at the Old Bailey in connection with the conspiracy to murder Queen Elizabeth and place Mary Queen of Scots on the Throne.

Many were the victims of this conspiracy. Men of wealth and

position were charged with plotting to assassinate Elizabeth, attempting to deliver Mary Stuart out of custody, procuring foreign enemies to invade the realm, and inciting an insurrection to join the enemy.

The conspirators were wont to meet in old St Paul's, St Giles Fields, and at certain taverns where they indulged in "entertainments, encouraged each other, and gloried in the enterprise they were about to undertake". But the scheme went astray through the vanity of some of the adventurous youngsters and in due course they were lodged in Newgate Gaol. Here they were kept until the day of the trial at the Old Bailey Sessions House.

They mostly pleaded guilty to high treason, and were quickly sentenced to death. There was little delay between the passing of sentence and its carrying out, for within ten days they set out from Newgate on their last earthly journey. Not to Tyburn this time, but to St Giles Fields where special gallows had been set up.

The execution was particularly barbarous; probably to act as a deterrent to all those who would plot and scheme against Elizabeth. Seven of the unhappy victims were cut down before they were dead. "Their Bowels were taken out with unusual Cruelty," says Camden. On the morrow, when six other conspirators were taken to St Giles Fields, Elizabeth ordered that "These shall have more mercy shewed them", and accordingly they were suffered to hang till they were dead before being disembowelled.

Precisely when the Sessions House became generally known as the Old Bailey, is not certain. Thomas Salmon, the erudite and prolific writer on geographical and historical subjects, referring to a case of high treason, describes it as "The Trial of Captain Thomas Lea, for High Treason at the *Old Baily*, London, the 26th Feb. 1600. 43 Eliz."

Salmon was the author of *A New Abridgement and Critical Review of the State Trials*, a voluminous work of 922 pages written at the beginning of the 18th century. Apart from his great travels—he had been round the world with Anson—he was a recognised authority on law, and his comments on the cases dealt with are as original as they are fearless.

The trial of Lea reveals the difference between the manner of treating a prisoner then and now. Lea was charged with "compassing and imagining the death of the Queen", and with "Endeavouring to persuade Sir Robert Crofts to assist in forcing the Queen to release the Earl of Essex, then a prisoner in the Tower."

The facts, briefly stated, are that Lea did certainly approach Crofts and suggest that Sir Walter Ralegh might earn himself "eternal honour and love" if he would procure Elizabeth's warrant to free Essex and the Earl of Southampton. Crofts said Sir Walter would not lend himself to any such scheme, but Lea replied that if six resolute men went into the Queen's apartment and knelt before her, saying they would not rise until she had signed the warrant and had the prisoners brought into her presence, this would have the desired effect. When asked what would happen if some of her Majesty's supporters "came upon them to remove them from the Queen's chamber", Lea is said to have answered:

"We might keep them out by shutting the door, and telling them that if harm came to the Queen, if she should do otherwise than well, be it at their peril."

Crofts reported this conversation, and close guard was kept upon the Queen's apartments. That evening, at dusk, Lea was seen by William Poynes outside the door of the Royal apartments, looking "pale, countenance stern, and great drops of sweat standing on his face".

Brought to trial in the Old Bailey, Lea's first act was to challenge one of the jurors. "But," says Salmon, "the Court told him they would not allow of such challenges; whereupon finding he was denied this piece of justice, he bid them proceed as they would."

From the outset the Attorney General showed bias against Lea. He read only part of the statement which the accused had made after arrest—that part where he said he loved and honoured the Earl of Essex as much as any man in England. When Lea demanded that the whole of his statement should be read, the Attorney General would not allow it.

In defence Lea declared that he never intended to take part in the enterprise, nor did he try to persuade any man to do so. He had merely spoken of it conditionally: "*If such a thing could be done.*" He pointed out that when he was found outside the Queen's Privy Chamber door, he had not so much as a dagger or any sort of arms about him, nor had he anybody with him, which might have shown that he intended to do Elizabeth harm. He also pointed out that he had been outside that same door five hundred times before without any notice being taken, had spent his blood in the Queen's service, and was ready to do so again.

The man Poynes, who saw Lea outside the door, was not called as a witness; his deposition was read in court. There can be little doubt that the jury had been well chosen and primed, for they were absent but a short time before they returned a verdict of Guilty.

Upon this the Attorney General urged Lea to confess, and tell the Court "who set him on". Lea hotly replied, "I am not a fool to be set on like a boy upon a bear. Nobody set me on, for I endeavoured nothing."

Observe the speed with which the law was applied when it was deemed necessary: Lea was brought to trial the day after his arrest in the palace and on the following day made the journey to Tyburn. He died bravely, protesting to the Minister to whom he freely confessed the rest of his sins, that he had never intended any harm to the Queen.

Salmon, commenting on this trial, remarks: "The Courts of Law, it appears, still acted very arbitrarily. For here we see the Judges denying the prisoner the benefit of his challenges which was his undoubted right. We find also Poyne's deposition read against him; whereas by Act of Parliament, the witnesses ought to have been produced in Court, face to face. And, without two such witnesses a man could not have been convicted of high treason. As for his own examination out of court, that could not have supplied the place of another witness unless he had confirmed it by a confession at his trial."

In view of these obvious points of law, it seems fairly clear that if there had been a Court of Criminal Appeal in the days of Elizabeth, Lea would not have died on the scaffold.

Newgate in 1800

From a print in the British Museum

CHAPTER FOUR

ST SEPULCHRE'S BELL OF DOOM

COURAGE in the face of death was fairly common in days of public executions, according to the records. Men and women alike displayed a worthy calm on the gallows, especially those who were victims of religious persecution.

A particularly pathetic instance was that of Mistress Anne Line (or Lynde) who, on 26 February, 1601, was charged at the Old Bailey with aiding the escape of a priest. A frail, slim widow, her strength sapped by the burning zeal with which she had devoted herself to the protection of priests, Anne Line had to be carried up the steep steps from the cells below, seated on a chair borne by two sturdy warders. There she sat, a silent figure, heedless of all that went on around her, while the evidence of her crime was marshalled with all the bigotry of which counsel was master. The jury found her Guilty, and on the following day she was carried to her execution.

The usual minister accompanied her on her last journey and on several occasions stopped the procession to urge "what meanes he could to persuade her to convert from her professed faithe and opinion". He "constantlie persevered therein", and when, at the foot of the gallows, he challenged her with having been "a common receavor of many priests", she replied in a firm voice, "Where I have receaved one I would to God I had receaved a thousand."

It is recorded that "she behaved herself most meekely patiently and vertuously to her last breath. She kissed the gallowes and before and after her private prayers blessing herself, the carte was drawne awaye, and she then made the signe of the crosse uppon her, and after that never moved."

At the same time were hanged two of the priests with whom she had been associated, Marke Barkworth and Roger Filcock. The chroniclers of that time were not too careful about names. We have Barkworth referred to as Mr Barkwey in the account of his execution. He is described as "coming to the hurdle (on which he was drawn to the gallows) praying and with a chearfull voyce and smylinge countenance singing all the way". He kissed the gallows and made the sign of the cross, then kissed the rope and again burst into a "chearfull" song. To the minister who bade him be penitent for his sins, he said, "Hold thy peace, thou arte a simple fellowe", and when reminded that Christ had died for him, he raised his pinioned hands aloft and answered, "And so do I for Him, and I would I had a thousand lyves to bestowe upon him in this cause." He continued to sign to the assembled crowds until the cart upon which he was standing was drawn away, "And beinge presently cut down, he stood uprighte on his feete and strugled with the Executioners cryinge, 'Lord, Lord, Lord', and being holden by the strengthe of the executioners on the hurdle dismembringe of him he cried 'Oh God' and so he was quartered."

Few of the landmarks which stood near the Old Bailey in the 17th century still exist.

The slums and the homes of the wealthy have gone. Gone too is the College of Surgeons and with it the Surgeons Hall to which the bodies of executed felons were taken for dissection. The College stood in the street of Old Bailey, almost next door to the gaol. Opposite what is now the main entrance of the Central Criminal Court was a large open space on which was held Newgate Market, a meat market which was used until 1861, when the wholesale marketing of meat was shifted to Smithfield.

In an old document of Cromwell's time, there is a description of how the lowing of herds of cattle being driven into Newgate market mingled with the clamour of the onlookers at the public executions and the strangled groans of the dying.

Smithfield (or Smoothfield), outside the City Wall, was famous in the 15th century as a jousting ground, and it is recorded how, in the year 1467, "the Bastarde of Burgoigne" did combat with Lord Scales, the joust lasting a full three days.

The grand old church of St Sepulchre's which fronts on to Holborn Viaduct, immediately across the road from the Old Bailey, was built in 1178, and still stands. It was given to the priors of St Bartholomew's the Great, only a stone's throw away in Giltspur Street, near to "Bart's" Hospital, of equal antiquity. Both church and hospital were founded by Rahere, the minstrel and favourite of Henry I, in 1123, but it is St Sepulchre's which has played so large a part in the annals of Newgate and the Old Bailey.

Up to 1890 one of its bells used to ring out the doom of condemned prisoners as they made their way to Tyburn or were hanged outside or within Newgate Gaol.

Robert Dow, Merchant Taylor of London, made a gift of £50 in 1604, in consideration "of the poore condemned prisoners in Newgate, where very often and very many of them after Judgement of Death, and at their very execution, remaine most carelesse of their Soules health, Jesting and deriding their imminent danger and to the Judgement of the world die reprobate". This worthy merchant, "the sayd Master Dow, hath given competent Maintenance for ever unto St Sepulchers parish for the towling of the great Bell and for some especiall man, by them to bee appointed to come to the sayd Prison, the midnight before execution, and then distinctly and solemnly to ring a hand bell; then to pronounce in a lowd voice at the prison gate, a Godly Christian remembrance of exhortation, appoynted by the Lorde Bishoppe, beginning thus:

'All you that in the condemned hole do lie,
Prepare you for to morrow you shall die

Watch all, and pray: the hour is drawing near
That you before the Almighty must appear.
Examine well yourself; in time repent
That you may not to eternal flames be sent.
And when St Sepulchre's Bell in the morning tolls
The Lord above have mercy on your souls.
Past 12 o'clock.' "

A nosegay was given the prisoners as they passed the church.

A copy of the above somewhat melancholy oration can be seen to-day hanging on the wall of St Sepulchre's Church. In a glass case on another wall is the hand-bell which the bell-man or sexton used to ring as he recited the following admonition:

"You prisoners that are within
Who for wickedness and sin,
After many mercies shown you, are now appointed to die tomorrow in the forenoon, give ear and understand that tomorrow morning the greatest bell of St Sepulchre's shall toll for you in form and manner of a passing bell as used to be tolled for those at point of death; to the end that all Godly people hearing that bell, and knowing that it is for you going to your deaths, may be stirred up heartily to pray to God to bestow his grace and mercy upon you while you live. I beseech you for Jesus Christ's sake to keep this night in watching and prayer for the salvation of your own souls . . ."

The bell-man was to give "twelve solemn tolls with double strokes", and was to receive the sum of £1 6s. 8d. a year. When the prisoners passed the church on their way to Tyburn in the morning, as the cart on which they were borne came into view from the gaol, the bell-man looked over the church wall, and called once more on prisoners and onlookers alike to pray, with the following exhortation:

"All good people pray heartily unto God for these

poor sinners who are now going to their death, for whom this great bell doth toll.

"You that are condemned to die, repent with lamentable tears; ask mercy of the Lord for the salvation of your souls through the merits, death and passion of Jesus Christ who now sits on the right hand of God, to make intercession for as many of you as penitently return unto him.

Lord have mercy upon you
Christ have mercy upon you
Lord have mercy upon you
Christ have mercy upon you."

Executions were an occasion for crowds of jeering or cheering men, women and children to follow the prisoners on their last journey from Newgate to Tyburn, and the record telling of the above custom naïvely adds: "But upon those occasions the noise is generally so great that nobody can hear a word that the bell-man says."

At one time the bell-man found himself with the melancholy duty of making the exhortation to his own vicar, one John Rogers, who was "kept amongst thieves and murderers for a great space" in Newgate, charged with heresy. Condemned by the Catholic Bishop of Winchester, he was first degraded and then taken to Smithfield, there to be burned at the stake as were all heretics in those days. Foxe, author of the *Book of Martyrs*, describes the vicar's journey to the place of doom.

"His wife and children, eleven in number, ten able to go and one at the breast, met him as he passed. This sorrowful sight of his own flesh and blood could nothing move him, but that he constantly and cheerfully took his death with wonderful patience in the defence and quarrel of Christ's Gospel."

Not every prisoner was convicted in those dark days, nor were all juries so heedless of their oaths that they brought in a verdict according to instructions. One man who was tried at the Old Bailey, and found Not Guilty by a courageous panel of his fellow-men, was Lieut.-Col. John Lilburn in 1653. He was charged with "felony in returning to England" after an "Ordinance by the Usurpers made for his Banishment".

The trial lasted four days and the verdict of Not Guilty was so popular that the cheers, when it was made known outside the Sessions House, could be heard "an English mile away" it was said.

Lilburn's offence was his attempted recovery of a coalmine in the County of Durham, for his Uncle George Lilburn and a Mr Josiah Primate for whom he was acting as solicitor. This colliery was worth about £5,000 a year, and had been taken by force from the two plaintiffs by Sir Arthur Haslerig.

Colonel Lilburn petitioned Parliament for justice, but Sir Arthur was so influential in the Long Parliament that he gained a favourable report. The petition of Lilburn was declared to be "false Malicious and scandalous", and it was stated that Sir Arthur had not been guilty of oppression or tyranny. An order was made that the petition should be burnt by the hangman, and that Mr Primate should pay £7,000 to the Commonwealth or lie in prison until it was paid. Colonel Lilburn was ordered to pay a fine of £3,000 to the Commonwealth, £2,000 to Sir Arthur Haslerig, and £2,000 to the Commissioners for "compounding with the delinquents".

In addition the Colonel, who had acted in a purely business capacity, was banished out of England, Ireland and Scotland "and the territories thereto belonging", it being a felony for him to return.

This aroused great indignation among many highly placed city people and others, who joined in a petition to Parliament praying that the sentence should be revoked, and that the parties concerned should be allowed to prosecute their cause at Law. But Parliament took no notice, and the Colonel crossed to Amsterdam. In June of the same year, however, he returned to Dover, was arrested, and brought to trial at the Old Bailey.

It was a remarkable trial in many ways. Five times in all he was brought to trial, the proceedings being adjourned because of the obvious state of public opinion in favour of the accused. "Freeborn John" they called him, and he certainly conducted his defence with all the dignity and courage of a freeborn man. Invited to plead Guilty or Not Guilty, he refused, complaining of the insufficiency and illegality of the indictment. It would be no good to point out errors after pleading, he told the court. He also asked for a copy of the indictment, which was denied him, as was his request that counsel should be assigned to him.

At length he did receive a copy of the indictment, and made out a list of his exceptions to the statements contained therein. The Court refused to accept these exceptions unless signed by his counsel. Lilburn pointed out that counsel had only been assigned to deal with one point, whereas there were several pleas he desired to make, pleas and exceptions which his counsel dare not sign. He realised that "the greatest men now in England were his adversaries", he told the court, and that his counsel, who were men of estate and practice, would be ruined if they argued on his behalf.

In the end he made an eloquent and cogent speech in his own defence, stating that, "If you deny me justice and will not let me speak for my life, I appeal to all the people who heard me this day, to know that the Lord Mayor, and the Court have robbed me of my birthright, and will not suffer me to speak for my life."

Salmon adds that, "Being master of very good lungs, he perfectly drowned the prosecutors and abused the Recorder Steel and the Attorney General Prideaux very handsomely; and when the court tried to browbeat and silence him, he cried out again, 'My Lord, will you murder me without law?' "

There is little doubt that Lilburn's appeal to the people made a strong impression on the Court, and Thurloe in his *State Papers* declares that even Cromwell was afraid of him. During the Colonel's trial three extra regiments were kept under arms at St James'.

Inside the Court were massed the supporters of the prisoner, some 700 strong, armed with pistols, swords and daggers, ready to create trouble if any verdict other than Not Guilty were returned. But the jury were swept away by the eloquence of the prisoner, and his brave demeanour throughout his trial. Although they were afterwards summoned before the Council of State and examined with regard to their verdict of Not Guilty, none of them suffered punishment.

Even so, the verdict of Not Guilty was of little use to him, for, as Salmon says: " . . . the Nation was governed with a Rod of Iron, and since they could not get him condemned in Courts of Law, they made use of pure Force and detained this rough Member of the Church Militant in Prison to his dying Day".

While in Newgate, Lilburn turned Quaker, in spite of his militant career. After his death his body was brought to the Quakers' meeting house at the *Bull and Mouth*, where it was put in a plain coffin without any pall, and thence carried, in contradiction to ancient custom, with the head foremost to the new churchyard at Bethlehem. There was no Christian burial or any ceremony; no mourning but the sighs of the Brethren.

Seven years later came one of the most important trials ever staged in the Old Bailey—the trial of the regicides.

It was a remarkable trial, for the prisoners were mainly those who had sat in judgment on King Charles I, and passed sentence of death upon him, while the judges who presided were for the most part those who had supported the Royalist party.

There were one or two exceptions, among them being the Duke of Albemarle, Lord Saye and Sele, the Earl of Shaftesbury and others. Now, with beautiful impartiality, they were prepared to sit in judgment upon their former friends and comrades.

The number of judges outnumbered the prisoners by five, for there were 29 of the latter and 34 of the former. The fact that Sir Heneage Finch, Solicitor-General, who now prosecuted, had previously been on the Commonwealth side with the prisoners, but now revealed a bitter animosity to his one-time comrades in the dock, is enough to show that opportunists will arise in every age.

Reference to this somewhat ironic position was made by Thomas Harrison, one of the prisoners, when on his own behalf he told the Court, "You know what a contest hath been in these nations for many years. Divers of those that sit upon the bench were formerly as active——" but he was allowed to get no further, for the Court intervened with a quick, "Pray Mr Harrison do not reflect upon the Court. This is not the business."

Later on, when Harrison argued that what had been done by himself and the other prisoners had been done on the authority of Parliament, "and whereas it hath been said we did assume and usurp authority, I say this was done rather in fear of the Lord", the Lord Chief Baron who was presiding answered wrathfully:

"Away with him. Know where you are Sir; you are in the assembly of Christians. Will you make God the author of your treason and murder?"

Solicitor-General Finch also added his comment.

"Though my lords have been pleased to give you a great latitude, this must not be suffered that you should run into these damnable excursions to make God the author of this damnable treason committed."

Prisoner after prisoner was charged, and made his separate defence, but the Sheriffs had done their work well. Anxious to gain favour with the judges, they had seen to it that the juries were packed with men who would return the verdict they were told to return. All the regicides were found Guilty and sentenced to be hanged, drawn and quartered.

For five days the executions went on. They were so brutally carried out that after ten of the "traitors" had met a terrible death, public feeling was aroused and King Charles II was urged to reprieve the remainder.

Colonel Thomas Harrison was the first to meet his fate, at "the Round or railed place near Charing Crosse".

He was dragged on a hurdle past the spot in Whitehall where Charles I had suffered beheading. On reaching the gallows, he found himself in the presence of thousands of people, including King Charles II himself, surrounded by many nobles and ladies of the Court.

The usual clamour broke out as Harrison was "turned off", and he had hanged for but a short time when the executioner cut down his still conscious body, and began to draw the intestines from his victim's stomach. These were cast into a brazier nearby, and then the quartering of the body rang down the curtain on this momentous tragedy.

Even then the full refinement of torture had not been reached, for when John Cook and Hugh Peters—Members of the Long Parliament and foes of the King—were trundled from Newgate the next day, the head of the butchered Harrison was placed on the hurdle of Cook, as it was dragged to Tyburn, and the unhappy Peters was secured to the rails of the gallows, and there compelled to look on while all the enormities of mutilation were performed upon his comrade.

Small wonder that the public, used as they were to look upon hangings as entertainment, revolted at these sights; particularly as a special Act had been passed by Parliament promising indemnity against punishment.

A report of that time states: "And now the stench of their burnt bowels had so putrefied the air, as the inhabitants thereabout petitioned His Majesty there might no more be executed in that place (Charing Cross)."

The reprieve of all but ten of the prisoners was only a temporary lull, for in 1662 four other regicides were hanged at Tyburn.

In 1660 a terrible vengeance had been wreaked on the remains of Cromwell, Ireton and Bradshaw, whose bodies had been buried with all honours in Westminster Abbey. On December 4 of that year a resolution was passed in the House of Commons, with an addition by the Lords, which demanded that the carcasses of the three above named should be taken from their graves, drawn to Tyburn and there hanged up in their coffins, and afterwards buried under the gallows.

Sir George Wharton in his *Gesta Britannorum* describes the scene:

"The odious carcasses of O. Cromwell, H. Ireton and J. Bradshaw drawn upon sledges to Tyburn, and being pulled out of their coffins, there hang'd at the several Angles of that Triple Tree till Sunset. Then taken down, beheaded, and their laothsome Trunckes thrown into a deep hole under the Gallowes. Their heads were afterwards set upon Poles on the top of Westminster Hall."

Thousands of those who had seen Cromwell in all his pride and power witnessed the desecration of his dead body.

Turning from these political trials, let us see how ordinary criminals fared at the 17th century Old Bailey.

I have often wondered, while listening to the trial of some modern adventuress, how any man could fall to her lure, or be taken in by the story she told. And I have often wondered what it was about Mary Moders, Stedman, Carleton, von Volway (to give but a few of her aliases) that caused men, young and old alike, to fall desperately in love with this ruthless 17th century trickster, and sacrifice themselves to her cupidity. Was it the generosity with which she distributed her favours? Was it her culture—she was certainly well read in the books of that day—or was it just the plain fact that wherever there is a woman, susceptible men are always to be found?

I do not pretend to know what was the power that Mary wielded (her trial took place in 1663), but never did a more spectacular adventuress enter the dock at the Old Bailey. Mary was the daughter of a chorister at Canterbury Cathedral, and achieved notoriety as "The German Princess".

Of a romantic turn of mind when young, she steeped herself in such stories as *Parismus and Parismenus*, and *Amadis de Gaul*; rather fancying herself as the character Oriana in the latter. Her first marriage was to a humble shoemaker by whom she had two children, both of whom died. Had they lived we might have had no story to tell. As it was, she yearned for the good things of life. When her first husband failed to supply them, she eloped to Dover where she bigamously married a surgeon, heedless of the fact that she already had a husband. The bigamy was discovered and she was arrested and brought to trial. For some unrecorded reason, the court acquitted her. She then took a trip to Holland and journeyed on to Cologne, where she took lodgings in a "house of entertainment", and lived in great splendour.

While there, she met an old gentleman of vast estates and wealth, who fell violently in love with her, as dotards have been known to do throughout history. He loaded her with valuable jewels and presents, and pressed her to marry him. At length, realising that he would not be put off much longer, she arranged to leave the district. She sent her landlady, with whom she had shared her lover's gifts, to make arrangements for the flight, and while the landlady was out of the way, broke open a chest in which she knew the latter kept her treasures. She decamped with a very fine haul. Her elderly lover had already given her a large sum of money with which to prepare for her wedding with him. Via Utrecht, Amsterdam, and Rotterdam, Mary fled to England, arriving at Billingsgate early one morning.

There she entered the Exchange Tavern for breakfast, to

find a number of young gentlemen of obvious wealth. Seeing a woman come unattended into a tavern so early in the morning, they imagined she was one of a certain class. They addressed her as such, upon which the artful Mary forced some tears to trickle down her cheeks, protesting that they would not treat a lady so if they knew that her father, the Lord Henry von Volway, a Prince of the German Empire, had banished her because she had fallen in love with a nobleman of whom he disapproved. The young gentlemen were duly touched by her tears and begged her to accept all the money they had upon them, with a promise to see her again. They did so, and it was at this period that Mary became known as "The German Princess".

It so happened that the Exchange Tavern was kept by a Mr King, who had married the sister of one John Carleton. John was introduced to the "princess" and immediately laid siege to her affections in the most extravagant manner. At length, with apparent reluctance, the "princess" consented to wed her lover of common blood. The ceremony took place, Carleton rejoicing in the possession of his regal bride, and Mary looking out for a suitable opportunity to escape with all the money and jewels she could.

Before anything of this kind could happen, however, an anonymous letter was received by Mr King, Carleton's brother-in-law. It was one of those documents we should to-day designate a poison-pen letter. It mentioned that the "German princess" was neither German nor a princess, and went on to say, "she has already married several men in our County of Kent . . . That you may be certain I am not mistaken in the woman, please to observe she has very high breasts, a very graceful appearance and speaks several languages fluently."

As a means of identification this description would not be acceptable in any Court of law to-day, but Mary Moders, alias Stedman, came before the Recorder at the Old Bailey, where with infinite aplomb she scuttled the prosecution by admitting the marriage to Carleton, but denying that she had ever been married to anybody named Stedman.

The Criminal Record Department of that day, or its equivalent, was not so efficient in keeping a list of previous convictions as our present-day department. Nothing was mentioned about the other marriage to the surgeon at Dover. A witness was brought to say that he had seen the first husband, Stedman, the week before the trial, and that Stedman would have come up to give evidence against the accused, but wanted money for the journey.

Mary thereupon declared that the prosecution was promoted by her father-in-law and her husband, because she refused to make over to the latter the fortune she possessed. She insisted that she was a foreigner, and that Carleton, believing her to be a woman of substance, had "solicited her with the greatest importunity" until she married him. He was in so much haste to get her fortune, she told the court, that he first of all married her without a licence, there being a further ceremony a few days later. She insisted that when she refused to comply with the demands of the father, he and his son had fabricated the story about her marriage to Stedman. She pointed out that no certificate of marriage had ever been produced.

Her arguments were so forceful that the court told the jury they must not condemn a person on hearsay. No reliable witness had been brought to testify to her having been married or having had children, and that if they found her Guilty, she must die.

"Whereupon the jury acquitted her," states the record.

Naturally she had received a certain notoriety as a result of her trial and the adventuress was quick to make the most of it. She obtained a theatrical engagement, appearing variously as a jilt, a coquette, and a chamber-maid, and also in a play *The German Princess* based on her story. At least two young bloods of that day came under her spell, and lavished presents upon her in much the same way as did the stage door "johnnies" in the old Gaiety days.

She went to live with a very old gentleman who gave her jewels and presents of money. One night when she had put him to bed in a state of intoxication, she rifled his pockets and belongings of every valuable she could find, and next appeared in another neighbourhood as a single woman whose uncle had provided her with a fortune of some thousand pounds.

Her enterprising landlady promptly foisted her nephew upon the wary "princess" who, ever on the look-out for another dupe, cunningly devised a scene worthy of a modern film setting. She arranged for a porter to deliver a letter to her while in the presence of her lover. On opening the letter she feigned a swoon, crying, "I am undone! I am undone!" The nephew, taking the letter, found that it purported to give news of the death of her brother who had left her a fortune; and to say that her father (who had banished her) was on his way over with a man whom he was determined she should marry. The ardent lover at once suggested she take shelter in his home, which she did, only to leave quietly in the night with all the valuables available.

Swindling tradesmen all over the place, she even played a version of what is known in modern crook slang as the badger trick on a youthful but wealthy young lawyer. Summoning him to her lodgings to discuss putting her estate out of reach of a mythical spendthrift husband with whom she was not living, the "princess" arranged the timely appearance of the "husband" on the scene. He burst open the wardrobe, in which she had persuaded the lawyer to hide on the pretext that she feared what her jealous husband might do if he found the lawyer in the room. The lawyer tried to explain the position, but the "husband" expressed violent disbelief, and eventually went off with £100 which had been extorted from the lawyer.

Not long afterwards the acquisitive Mary stole a silver tankard from a tavern in Covent Garden, and this time, when charged, she was not so successful in impressing the jury. She was found Guilty, but the sentence of death was afterwards commuted to one of transportation for life.

Behold her, then, aboard ship with the scum of the criminal world, bound for Jamaica. One might have thought this would have ended the career of this amazing adventuress. Nothing of the kind! On arrival in the West Indies, she exercised her wiles to such an extent that she managed to escape and board a ship bound for England. As soon as she landed, she set up as an heiress.

But Nemesis awaited her.

It so happened that a brewer of Southwark had been robbed of a sum of £200 (nothing to do with Mary) and asked a Mr Lowman, keeper of the gaol at Marshalsea, Southwark, to scour all the suspicious houses in the neighbourhood.

In the course of his search, Lowman happened on a house in New Spring Gardens, where he saw a "gentlewoman" walking up some stairs in her nightgown. He followed her into a room, and noticed three letters which he began to examine. The lady became extremely angry, and challenged his right to tamper with her letters, whereupon the gaoler, scrutinising her more closely, exclaimed, "You're the German Princess." He had recognized her because she had been in his charge when she was awaiting trial before. He knew she had been sentenced to transportation, and knew she had no right to be back in the country. So back to Marshalsea went Mary, to appear at the Old Bailey for the last time.

She gave the Court quite a lot of trouble, raising first this point and then another. When all else failed she declared that she was an expectant mother, but a jury of matrons, summoned to the spot, soon put an end to this fiction and the German Princess was at length sentenced to death.

On the day of her execution, she was "gay and brisk". When her irons had been removed (for she was shackled) she pinned a picture of husband Carleton to her sleeve, and then, as she

St Sepulchre's in the early 19th century

From a print in the British Museum

rode past St Sepulchre's Church, gave a mild oration.

It is recorded that she comported herself with dignity and courage during the last moments of her life. She was buried in the churchyard of St Martin's Church, that picturesque old building half-way up Ludgate Hill, whose bell used to toll the curfew when London was a walled City.

A wit of that day wrote her epitaph:

> "*The German Princess, here against her will,*
> *Lies underneath, and yet, oh strange, lies still.*"

CHAPTER FIVE

HIGH TREASON AND HIGHWAYMEN

THE inventive faculty of crooks in making up some acceptable story of how they came by stolen articles, has not developed much through the ages. Thieves and receivers have ever displayed a pathetic lack of originality in their explanations. I have often sat in the Old Bailey and marvelled to hear the same old tale trotted out by a prisoner.

He was, he says, enjoying a quiet cup of tea at a coffee-stall, when a complete stranger came up, and handing him a parcel, asked him to "mind this" for a few minutes. The man then vanished, did not come back, and the accused took the parcel home in all innocence, hoping to happen across the trusting acquaintance at some later date.

Occasionally the story varies. The stolen property was handed to the accused by a trusting gentleman whom he only knew as "Joe", and who promised to come back and collect it later, but never did. No, he did not know where "Joe" lived, nor what was his surname; and he had never seen him since.

A similar story, but with a different twist, was told by Colonel James Turner, "a man who lived in Credit and Reputation in the City", according to Salmon, the writer and commentator on State Trials. In this case Turner and his whole family, which included a wife and three children, stood in the dock at the Old Bailey in 1663, charged jointly with burglary. The victim was a Mr Tryon, friend of the family, who was robbed of jewellery, gold and over £1,000 in cash.

Turner protested his innocence, saying that his whole household were in bed when the robbery was committed, and that when the Sheriff—who suspected him—told him of the robbery, he had at once gone to give assistance to the burgled Mr Tryon.

As a result of this visit, said Turner, he went in search of a man named John Wild, found him, challenged him with having committed the crime, and promised him immunity from arrest if he would return the stolen property. Wild said he would do this, and in fact brought the money to his (the prisoner's) house, saying that he would bring the rest later on. But, said Turner, his arrest prevented the restitution of the remaining missing articles.

It was a good story but for the fact that evidence was called proving that Turner had persuaded some friends in the Minories to hide the money in their house. He was found Guilty and sentenced to death, the remainder of his family being acquitted.

While he was telling his story, Turner's wife dared to interrupt her lord and master, but he promptly crushed her with a bland "Prythee Mall, sit down and do not put me out. You see, my Lord, my wife will interrupt me with nonsense . . . I have had 27 children by her, 15 sons and 12 daughters."

I do not know if he mentioned this by way of mitigation. If so, it did not have the desired affect.

Turner was one of those miscreants who loved to hear himself talk and when at length he reached the gallows he indulged himself to the full. His oration opened with a harangue to the sheriffs in which he generously forgave those who had brought him to this end; he next complained of the "hole" where he had been confined the night after sentence had been passed on him. It certainly seems to have been an unpleasant place, but I fancy that any death cell has little to recommend it.

"It is a most sad deplorable place," declared Turner. "Hell itself, in comparison cannot be such a place; there is neither bench, stool nor stick for any person there; they lie like swine upon the ground, one upon another howling and roaring . . ."

At length his oration was over, and the hangman began to adjust the rope, but Turner had not done with his complaints. "What, dost thou intend to choke me?" he demanded. "Pray fellow give me more rope; what a simple fellow is this! How long have you been executioner that you know not where to put the knot?''

And then, when offering to pull down himself the cap placed over his head as a condemned man, he espied a pretty gentlewoman at a window, and gallantly kissed his hand to her as he cried, ''Your servant, Mistress.'' The next moment he was ''turned off'' but to his last breath, it is said, remained undaunted.

The latter half of the 17th century is one of the darkest periods in the history of London, and of Newgate and the Old Bailey. The Great Fire of London caused much havoc in 1666, and both Newgate Gaol and the Old Bailey Sessions House suffered damage. Neither was completely burnt down nor demolished, as so many historians have stated, but the damage was enough to necessitate the repair of the old prison, which was made stronger and more convenient, with a postern for foot passengers on either side of the main gate.

On the city side of the building three stone statues were set up, representing Justice, Mercy and Truth. On the side looking out towards Holborn, were Liberty (with Whittington's cat lying at her feet), Peace, Plenty and Concord. Four of these figures survived the Gordon Riots in 1780, when the prison was set on fire by the rioters, and continued to ornament the rebuilt gaol until it was finally demolished in 1902. I have tried to trace the whereabouts of these figures since that time, but have not been able to do so.

They were bought by Holloway & Co., Ltd., the firm which carried out the demolition work, but apparently no record was kept of what happened to them after that.

The courage of the citizens of London in facing the destruction of homes and belongings in the Great Fire, is only equalled by the courage of Londoners of more recent years, whose homes were fired and destroyed by Hitler's airmen.

The Fire of London victims had other things to suffer besides the material loss. They had to put up with a resumption of the cruel purge of men whose religious beliefs did not coincide with those of the particular party in power. There was another spate of trials for high treason. No fewer than thirteen priests were hanged, drawn and quartered, for no other "crime" than that of being priests. In the three years, 1678-1681, there were sixteen people sentenced to death, including the five Jesuit priests with whose parody of a trial I dealt with briefly in the opening chapter of this book, in connection with the Popish Plot.

In addition, eight more priests were hanged during that same period, under the newly revived penal laws which made it a capital offence for a Catholic priest to be in England.

For years, misgovernment under Charles II had produced such misery that people all over the country were near breaking point. The politicians of that day had played on the fears of the people by insinuating that the French were about to send an invading army to our shores to impose upon them the religion of the Pope. They emphasised their propaganda by pointing out that there was no successor to the king except his brother the Duke of York, a fervent Catholic.

About this time Titus Oates and Dr Ezrael Tonge came on the scene. Between them they evolved the story of a sinister plot on the part of the Papists to murder the King and massacre his supporters, as a first move to enslave the country.

But despite their plausibility, little credence was given to the story, until Sir Edmondbury Godfrey, a magistrate who had taken the depositions of Oates and Tonge on this alleged plot, suddenly vanished. Some days later his body was found impaled upon a sword which turned out to be his own.

The scheming pair promptly put it around that Godfrey had been murdered by the Papists. They said that he had been inveigled into Somerset House and there set upon by three men, who had afterwards dumped the body at the foot of Primrose Hill, where it was subsequently discovered.

There is not a single historian of any note who agrees that

the three men who were tried, convicted and hanged for this crime, had anything whatever to do with it. They were convicted on the perjured evidence of Titus Oates, William Bedloe, Miles Prance and others, all of whom were professional witnesses.

Prance told a most circumstantial story of how he had seen Green, one of the accused, first strangle Godfrey, and, finding him still alive, he "wrung his neck right round". Then, after they had deposited the body in this place and that place, said Prance, "about twelve on Wednesday night they carried it in a Sedan through the great gate of the upper court of Somerset House to Soho, where Hill met them with a horse, and setting the body upon the horse, Hill rode behind it".

Lord Shaftesbury was at the head of the political party who were concerned to exploit the death of Godfrey as part of a Popish plot and, having succeeded in getting their innnocent victims done to death, they continued to employ Oates, Bedloe and company, who gave evidence against other victims.

We are not so much concerned here with the victims of this deliberate judicial murder (they were not tried at the Old Bailey) but the circumstances of the trial were similar to those at the trial of the Five Jesuits, about which I want to give a few more details.

Thomas White (or Whitebread) head of the English Jesuits; Williams Harcourt, Rector of London; John Fenwicke, Procurator for the English Jesuits; John Gavan (or Gawen) and Anthony Turner, Popish priests and Jesuits, were all charged with high treason.

I have shown how, on being arraigned, White and Fenwicke protested that they had already been tried on the same charge, and that the jury had found the evidence to be insufficient. To-day, that would have entitled the prisoners to a verdict of Not Guilty and an acquittal—and rightly so. But you will recall how the Lord Chief Justice, Scroggs, brushed aside the claim of the prisoners that they should not be put in jeopardy of their lives a second time.

Titus Oates, despite having taken Holy Orders, and wearing his canonical robes, did not hesitate to give perjured evidence. He was responsible for sending scores of innocent people to a terrible death. You will remember how sixteen witnesses were brought from St Omer, to say that they saw and talked with Oates in France at the very time he declared he was in England. To this Oates replied that the witnesses were Papists and Jesuits, and would swear anything for their cause. Lord Chief Justice Scroggs backed him up by observing that while Papists were competent witnesses in law, "yet they were of such principles that the jury ought to give them little credit".

But he was even stronger in his summing-up, for he told the jury outright that the testimony of the witnesses from St Omer was of much less weight than that which had been given on the other side, *because the testimony of a Papist was not to be credited with or without oath.*

Again and again throughout the trial, both judge and witnesses derided the value of any testimony given on behalf of the prisoners. There was a touch almost of malevolence in of final strictures of Scroggs when he described the St Omer witnesses as people who "had practised all sorts of lying and equivocation" and declared that their "dispensations, pardons and indulgencies for breach of vows rendered them unfit for human society, or to have any faith or credit given to their testimony".

The next day there entered the same dock Richard Langhorn, charged with high treason, aiding and abetting three other men in a traitorous plan to kill the King, and a few other counts. Again Titus Oates and Bedloe gave evidence, which was challenged by the prisoner. He declared that Bedloe had received a sum of £500 for his evidence, and that Oates had been proved a liar when he said he was present at the "consult" in April, 1678. Langhorn said that if Oates was a perjurer in this, his other evidence could not be believed.

Again the Lord Chief Justice came to the rescue. Regarding

Bedloe's payment for testimony, he said it was a reflection on the integrity and wisdom of the King to suggest that the offering of a reward for evidence rendered that evidence worthless. He further told the jury that "the plot was proved as clear as the day" by Oates's testimony.

The five Jesuits and Langhorn were all found Guilty and were all brought together for sentence at the same time. It was the custom for the Chief Justices to sum up to the jury, and then, when the latter had given their verdict it was the Recorder of the City of London who passed sentence.

At that time, the Recorder was a young lawyer named George Jeffreys. He latter attained notoriety as Judge Jeffreys of the "Bloody Assizes". I mention him at this point, because, when the jury found the five priests guilty of high treason, Jeffreys commented that he "*thought every honest man would say they were unexceptionally found so. It was a just verdict the jury had given.*"

The Recorder seemed to consider it an occasion to enlarge. He expatiated on the heinousness of the crimes of which the six prisoners had been found Guilty. He decried the "bloody principles on which their religion was founded", and then went on: "The crimes have been so fully proved that no person here can have any doubt of your guilt. There is not the least reason to suspect the credibility of the witnesses produced against you."

That was in the year 1679, and the irony of that quotation lies in the fact that six years later, in the reign of James II, Titus Oates appeared before Jeffreys—who by that time was Lord Chief Justice—on charges of perjury, one of the indictments being "That the said Titus Oates at the trials of Fenwick and Whitebread (White) and other Jesuits, did falsely swear and give evidence to the jury who tried that cause . . . and so the said Titus Oates did commit wilful and corrupt perjury."

During this later trial Jeffreys described Oates as "the most impudently hardened wretch that I ever saw". And later in his summing-up he had the bold face to declare:

"Every person that has been executed for the Popish Plot, truly called Oates plot, did to a man deny it at their deaths and took it upon their salvations they were innocent." He went on to say that lying was as much "the talent of the Presbyterian as it was of a Papist. Nay (it was an inseparable incident to a Presbyterian) and such snivelling, canting, whining knaves, to lie as it was to speak . . . The nation was in a hurry and surprise (when it dealt with the Papists) *and it was not then supposed that there could be such villains upon earth as impudently to swear high treason against their fellow-subjects when there was no truth in the accusation* . . . But we should use our most urgent endeavours to inflict the greatest vengeance that the justice of the nation can permit us to inflict upon such villains, who have contracted so much mischief and reproach upon us, and so much guilt upon themselves."

How glibly these judicial monsters misused the word Justice, and how easily were juries swayed one way or the other by the unctuous phrases of those who sat in judgment on their fellow creatures! This jury was absent only half-an-hour before returning a verdict of Guilty. Jeffreys' determination that the greatest vengeance should be wreaked upon Oates, was certainly carried into effect by Recorder Wythens, who passed the following sentence:

"That he should stand in the pillory before Westminster Hall Gate for an hour with a paper over his head declaring his crime, that on the following day he should stand in the pillory outside the Royal Exchange, and that on the next day he should be whipped from Aldgate to Newgate by the hands of the Common hangman, and two days later be whipped from Newgate to Tyburn.

"That on the 9th August every year of his life he should stand in the pillory before Westminster Hall Gate; on the 10th August at Charing Cross; on the 11th over against the Temple . . ."

There were other yearly occasions on which he was to stand in the pillory during his lifetime, but he was not called upon to suffer these punishments for long.

Few men in history ever suffered such a lashing as did Oates. Tied to the cart-tail, and dragged along amid a jeering, shouting crowd, he was flogged without mercy by the brawny hangman. An all too brief respite of forty-eight hours, and he was brought out from his Newgate cell and dragged to Tyburn, the hangman again plying his heavy thonged whip. For a long time on each of these journeys Oates stood the pain without murmur; but at length the agony broke down his resistance and he gave vent to piercing shrieks until a merciful unconsciousness seized him.

Taken back to Newgate, he was flung into a cell in which there was no glimmer of light, and there left for several months, bent beneath the weight of the irons with which he was shackled hand and foot.

"He received upward of two thousand lashes," wrote a chronicler of that day, adding, "Such a thing was never inflicted by any Jew, Turk, or heathen, but Jeffreys. Had they hanged him they had been more merciful; had they flayed him alive it is a question whether it would have been so much torture."

But Fate had another trick in store.

In September, 1688, Oates stood in the pillory before the Royal Exchange for the last time, for in 1689 a resolution was passed in the House of Commons "*that the prosecution of Titus Oates upon two indictments for perjury was a design to stifle the Popish Plot, and that the verdicts given thereupon were corrupt and that all judgments given thereupon were cruel and illegal*".

The Reformation had come about, and the accommodating Titus had become Protestant champion. He received a pardon, was set free, and was awarded a considerable pension.

In the meantime Judge Jeffreys had fallen foul of the new political and religious régime. James II had been forced to flee England in 1688 and was an exile in France. Jeffreys tried to make his escape thither in disguise, but was captured and sent to the Tower where he died a few months before Oates was set at liberty.

Let us leave high treason trials for the time being, and address ourselves to the more picturesque adventures of highwaymen, who, round about this time, began to flourish.

Few had so spectacular a career as Claude Duval, darling of the ladies, and so great a gallant in his depredations that he gave tone and dignity to his exploits.

As his name would suggest, Duval—or Du Vall, as he is called in official records—was of French extraction. His humble parents intended him to go into domestic service, but when he was about thirteen, he was turned adrift in the world, and started out from his birthplace in Normandy to see Paris.

At Rouen, he fell in with a number of English exiles who had been forced to flee England on account of their royalist sympathies. One of them was the Duke of Richmond, who brought young Claude over to England as footman.

Alas, high life appears to have upset the equilibrium of Duval, and he got into bad ways. The time was ripe for debauchery of all kinds. With the return of Charles II the populace generally, and those royalists who were able to return to their native land, celebrated with scenes of riotous merry-making. The wages of a footman did not run to excesses of this kind, with the result that Claude resorted to the hold-up of carriages and foot passengers on the highway, and found it a very lucrative sideline.

At length he decided to make highway robbery his career, and did so with such success that his name was placarded over the countryside, a proclamation being issued for his arrest.

The famous story of Duval's hold-up on Hampstead Heath may or may not be true, but it is typical of the character of the man, and explains why such an outlaw of society should have been so popular among the general public. It happens that a young and very beautiful woman, accompanied by her aged and wealthy husband, was crossing Hampstead Heath by carriage when Duval called to them to stand and deliver. The lady, to show she was unafraid, began to play upon a flageolet when the masked Claude appeared at the window of the carriage. With old world chivalry the highwayman remarked that he would wager his life so pretty a lady could dance as well as she played. He invited her out of the carriage onto the roadway, and there, in the moonlight, trod a coranto with his fair partner. It is said that the highwayman danced with a grace that would have done credit to a London dancing master, in spite of his heavy French riding boots.

At the end of the dance, he handed the lady back into the carriage; and then, as the husband gave orders for his coachman to drive off, Duval reminded him that he had not paid for his entertainment. The knight—for so report describes him—was doubtless so glad to get away with his life that he produced a bag containing one hundred pounds from under the seat. He handed this to Claude, who, with a sweep of his feathered hat, declared that a voluntary gift was worth ten times more than one taken by force, and consequently he would forgo the other £300 which he knew his victim was carrying.

At length the Law was so close on his heels that Duval decided to return to France for a time, and there carried on a further series of hold-ups to his great financial advantage.

On his next visit to England, Duval was not so fortunate. Early in 1670 he was captured at the *Hole in the Wall*, in Chandos Street, and taken to Newgate.

His appearance at the Old Bailey was the occasion of a great gathering of noblemen with their ladies, many of whom had been victims of the handsome Claude. Sentenced to death, he comported himself with admirable courage before the great concourse of people who gathered to witness his execution.

It is a singular thing, but the public, on the occasion of the hanging of a highwayman, invariably displayed the greatest sympathy with the victim of the rope, while they would jeer at prisoners hanged for other crimes.

After Duval had "hanged a convenient time," says one writer, "he was cut down, and, by persons well dressed, carried into a mourning coach, and so conveyed to the Tangier Tavern in St Giles, where he lay in state all that night, the room hung with black cloth, the hearse covered with escutcheons, eight wax tapers burning, and as many tall gentlemen with long black cloakes attending".

There seems to have been a weakness for taverns both in life and in death with Claude, and one gathers that the tall, black-cloaked gentlemen were either some of his brethren of the road, or else professional mourners, engaged for the purpose by the dead man's admirers. "Mum was the word," the narrator continues, "great silence expected from all that visited for fear of disturbing this lion. And this ceremony had lasted much longer had not one of the judges (whose name I must not mention here, lest he should incur the displeasure of the ladies) sent to disturb this pageantry."

Duval was not the only highwayman to hold court of society beauties in the death cell. This disposition on their part gave rise to some memoirs ascribed to William Pope, and entitled: *Intended as a Severe Reflexion on the too great Fondness of English Ladies towards French Footmen: which, at That Time of Day was a too common Complaint.*

According to this work—typically satirical if Pope was indeed the author—it is stated that on the tomb of Duval in St Paul's Church, Covent Garden, there is the following epitaph over which is emblazoned the family arms.

"Here lies Duval; reader if male thou art,
Look to thy purse; if female, to thy heart.
Much havoc hath he made of both, for all
Men he made stand, and women he made to fall.

The Second Conqueror of the Norman race,
Knights to his arms did yield, and ladies to his face.
Old Tyburn's glory, England's bravest thief,
Duval, the ladies joy: Duval, the ladies grief."

Not all highwaymen were as gallant and courtly as Claude Duval, and no more reprehensible specimen ever disgraced his profession than William Cady, son of a Norfolk surgeon. He went to Cambridge Unversity, took his B.A., and then, having practised medicine for a short spell, took to the road. He robbed Lord Viscount Dundee by a simple ruse. Sending the Viscount's footmen off in chase of a mythical footpad, Cady drew his pistols and at their point relieved the nobleman of his wealth.

A reward of £100 was offered in the *London Gazette* for his capture, but Cady fled to France and took refuge in a seminary, where he was soon listening to the confessions of penitents. After a while, as ecclesiastical discipline began to pale, he decided to return to England.

The need for money dictated his next move. Among those who attended him regularly in the confessional were two young and wealthy women, and he decided that they must contribute to his funds. One day when they entered his room, he held them up at the point of his pistols, robbed them of their money, rings and other jewellery, raped them, gagged them, tied them neck and heels and made off.

In England he held up a rich hop merchant named Sandal, and his wife; when Sandal made a fight of it, Cady shot his horse from under him, then tied him up so that he was helpless. He then demanded the woman's wedding ring from her finger. But she wept and begged him to let her keep it, as it possessed such great sentimental value.

"You whining bitch," quoth Cady, threatening to cut off the wife's finger unless she handed over the ring. Whereupon she drew it off, as though to hand it to him, popped it quickly into her mouth and swallowed it. Cady stamped and raved at being outwitted, and then, in an access of rage, shot the woman through the head. Before the eyes of her horrified and helpless husband he then ripped her up with a knife and took the ring from her mutilated body.

He was arrested after he had committed two other murders, shooting it out with his captors. Brought up at the Old Bailey, he was sentenced to death, and while in the condemned cell sang and swore, and roared, and got drunk.

On passing St Sepulchre's Church on the way to Tyburn, he rated the Sheriffs for detaining him to "hear an old puppy chatter nonsense".

CHAPTER SIX

INTRODUCING A HANGMAN

THE story of the trial of Lord William Russell, in 1683, has been written so many times that I only wish to touch upon it as an instance of the resolute manner in which men of sincere conviction faced death on the gallows.

Lord William was one of those charged with high treason in connection with what is known as the Rye House Plot. Rye House, near Hoddesdon, Hertfordshire, was the place where a number of people planned to murder Charles II and his brother James as they returned from Newmarket to London. From the first, Russell denied his guilt, and most historians are agreed that there is little proof of his ever having taken part in the plot.

A Whig in politics, he was a mild and tolerant Christian by religion. When he knew that he was to be questioned about his alleged part in the plot, he realised that he was doomed, even before his trial took place. He told his servant Taunton that "they would have his life", and when the faithful Taunton replied that he prayed his enemies would not have power to take it, his master replied, "Yes—the devil is loose."

Lord William was right. He had many friends in high places —the Duke of Monmouth and the Earl of Essex. They would have rallied to his aid, but Lord William declared that it would be of no advantage to him to have his friends die with him. He was tried, found Guilty, and sentenced to be hanged with all the usual disgusting accompaniments of the death sentence for treason.

The King later changed the sentence, and ordered him to be beheaded. Lord William had become a hero and martyr in the eyes of his supporters and many attempts were made to

Trial by Jury at the Old Bailey, 1809

From a coloured print by Rowlandson, published in 1809

save his life. His father, the Earl of Bedford, offered £50,000 for a pardon. The Duke of Monmouth used his best endeavours to persuade the King to change his mind. To the plea of the doomed man's father, the King replied, "If I do not take away his life, he will soon have mine."

Meanwhile, the central figure of this grim drama sat quietly in his Newgate cell awaiting death. His wife and children were daily visitors, together with his many friends. On the eve of his execution he begged his wife to stay with him a little later than usual.

"Stay and sup with me," he begged. "Let us eat our last earthly food together," and then, when it rained hard that night, "Such a rain to-morrow, will spoil a great show which is a dull thing on a rainy day."

As his wife took her leave, he held her hand fondly, and said, "This flesh you feel now, in a few hours must be cold." He kissed her four or five times, and so they parted in calm and tearless silence.

The next morning the Sheriffs appeared; Lord Russell left Newgate and entered his own coach, in which he was driven past his house to the special scaffold—shrouded in mourning—which had been erected in Lincoln's Inn Fields. As he reached the Fields, he was amazed to see such a huge crowd of people, and to observe the unusual silence. It was raining hard, and he turned to his companions in the carriage.

"This rain may do hurt that are bare-headed," he remarked, even in his last moments being thoughtful for others. Then he mounted the scaffold, made a short speech, and, removing his peruke, cravat and coat, laid his neck on the block, his lips moving in prayer.

The hangman missed at the first stroke, and ". . . severed his (Lord Russell's) head from his body at three strokes very barbarously".

Ketch, the executioner, made an even greater mess of things two years later when he was called upon to behead the Duke of Monmouth at Tower Hill. The Duke had heard reports of the hangman's bungling on the occasion of Russell's execution and, anxious to avoid a similar experience, he handed Ketch six guineas, remarking, "Pray do your business well; don't serve me as you did my Lord Russell. I have heard you struck him three or four times."

Then, turning to his servant, he handed him a bag of gold. "Here," he went on, "take these remaining guineas and give them to him if he does his work well." And then to Ketch, "If you strike me twice, I cannot promise not to stir."

The report goes on: "Then he lay down, and soon after raised himself upon his elbow and said to the executioner, 'Prithee, let me feel the axe', and felt the edge and said, 'I feel it is not sharp enough.' Then he lay down, the Divines praying earnestly for the acceptance of his repentance, and commended to God his soul and spirit. So the executioner did his work; but I hear he had five blows. So he died."

A laconic enough report.

Jack Ketch's callous brutality in the exercise of his office earned him such opprobium that for years after his death succeeding hangmen were nicknamed "Jack Ketch". Perhaps it was too much to expect a man to be good at hanging as well as beheading, not to mention the minor accomplishments of drawing and quartering, and impaling traitors' heads upon poles.

There were other duties, such as branding with a hot iron, ear-cropping, nose-slitting, whipping at the cart-tail, and other little pleasantries of punishment, and one cannot altogether blame the hangman for lacking the milk of human kindness, when he was ordered to whip a woman in the following words:

"Hangman, I charge you pay particular attention to this lady. Scourge her soundly man; scourge her till the blood runs down. It is Christmas—a cold time for madam to strip. See that you warm her shoulders thoroughly."

Those words were uttered by Lord Chief Justice Jeffreys, the handsome but sadistic judge of the "Bloody Assizes".

gruesome subject I turn to the etiquette of the gallows.

This was rigidly adhered to, and the "quality" were dealt with in strict order of precedence according to their rank, just as at a Royal or State function to-day. Thus, when the Duke of Hamilton, the Earl of Holland, and Lord Capel were beheaded, they were brought to the block in the order of their rank. And when Capel was about to make a speech with his hat on he was ordered to take it off.

Later, when the Earl of Kilmarnock offered to waive his right to make a speech, in favour of Lord Balmerino, the Sheriffs would not allow this breach of etiquette in any circumstances, and it was the Earl of Kilmarnock who harangued the crowd.

I have noticed that the same insistence on etiquette was not applied to the "lower orders". For example, when Sam Hall, the chimney sweep, of ballad fame, was riding in the cart to Tyburn, by his side was a notorious highwayman, complete in gay attire and fine nosegay. Sam lurched against him and the highwayman snapped out, "Stand off fellow—stand off!" But Sam was having none of this class distinction in his last hours, and promptly retorted, "Stand off yourself, fellow. I have as good a right to be here as you have!"

Edward Dennis, the hangman who was condemned for taking part in the No Popery riots in 1780, was afterwards reprieved and figures as one of the characters in Dickens' *Barnaby Rudge*.

But let us leave the hangman for the hanged, and return to the Old Bailey and the case of Tom Savage, a seventeen-years-old youth, who was to attain the unhappy fame of being twice hanged.

Tom must have been one of those problem boys we hear so much about these days. *Newgate Calendar* records that for two years after he reached the age of fifteen he "led a loose and profligate life".

The main cause of his downfall—according to the *Calendar*

—was that "Breaking the Sabbath, he never having once heard a whole service during that time, was the first inlet to his vices, especially whoredom, drunkenness and theft, for he used commonly to pass away the Sabbaths at a bawdy-house in Ratcliff Highway, with one Hannah Blay, a vile common strumpet, who was the cause of his ruin, and brought him to his shameful end."

Hannah was undoubtedly a "gold-digger", for she was always impressing upon Tom that unless he brought her money he could not enjoy her company; and if he could not get it by fair means he must steal it from his master. When Tom remonstrated that a maid was always present in the house, Hannah replied, "Hang her for a jade. Knock her brains out. Bring some money and I'll go away with you."

And poor, youthful, susceptible Tom did as he was told. He cruelly battered the maid's head in, and then ran off with a bag containing money belonging to his master. When he found Hannah only wanted the money, and was unwilling to risk any unpleasantness through association with him, Tom gave her half-a-crown, and went on the run. Remorse seized him and when overtaken he gladly unburdened himself of his crime, and as gladly confessed his guilt in the dock at the Old Bailey.

Condemned to death, he was visited in Newgate by a kindly friend, a Mr Baker, who was full of sympathy for the boy. Taking his friend by the hand, Tom conducted him to the place where the rough coffin in which he was to be buried was awaiting him.

"Here is the ship wherein I must launch out into the ocean of eternity," he said.

It was the custom in those days for the condemned to have this reminder ever before their eyes, and on the last Sunday before their execution, all those condemned to death gathered together in the prison chapel for the preaching of what was known as the "death sermon".

The public were admitted to the chapel, and occupied a

gallery from which they could look down on the poor devils congregated in a large oblong enclosure in the very centre of the chapel, where they sat at a table on which rested a large black coffin. Other felons occupied a few pews set aside for them, and privileged visitors were permitted to drape themselves around the death pen.

In due course Tom made his journey to Tyburn, a brave and reverent youth, unafraid to pay the penalty of his crime. He freely forgave the woman who had lured him into slaying the maid; he beseeched the crowd of onlookers to take heed of the waywardness which had brought him to his death, and then was turned off.

Had there been inquests after executions at that time, as there are to-day, it could not have been said that the execution was carried out without a hitch, for Tom Savage struggled and heaved until a friend beat him heavily on the chest to hurry the end. Then, after he had hung a considerable time, he was cut down and his body handed over to his friends who took it to a house nearby to prepare for burial.

Suddenly, it was noticed that there were signs of revival, and with anxious hands Tom was carried to a bedroom where he was placed in bed, and warm blankets applied. Very soon, the "corpse" began to show more definite signs of recovery, but in the meantime the news that he was not dead had reached the Sheriff's Officer, who came rushing round to collect young Tom. He was at once taken back to the same gallows and there hanged a second time, the hangman making quite sure that there was no mistake on this occasion.

There was in those days no law against a person being hanged a second time. Nor is there at present any law to prevent it if the occasion should arise, although I think it would be very unlikely. Of course there is the classic instance of John Lee, the Babbacombe murderer, who went thrice to the scaffold but did not die, and who thus earned for himself the soubriquet of The Man They Could not Hang. There was a difference, though, between the case of John Lee and that of Tom Savage.

Lee was sentenced to death in 1885 for the murder of Miss Emma Keyse, a wealthy woman occupying a beautiful house overlooking Babbacombe Bay. He was footman to his victim, and had battered in her head, soaked with paraffin the room in which she was found dead, and set the place ablaze.

Tried before Mr Justice Manisty, who gave a long and careful survey of the evidence, Lee remained calm throughout his trial, and when at length found Guilty and asked whether he had anything to say, replied quietly:

"The reason I am so calm and collected, my lord, is because I trust in the Lord. I am innocent."

At Exeter Gaol one February morning, Berry, the hangman, went to the cell to pinion the doomed man. Lee was still confident and assured. He followed the chaplain who was murmuring the usual prayers for the dead, and stood unflinchingly on the platform of death.

Overnight, Berry had satisfied himself that the scaffold was in perfect working order. Lee toed the chalk marks on the trapdoor, and Berry strapped his legs at the ankles. A few seconds later he pulled the lever. John Lee should have dropped through the platform into the pit below. But—he didn't. The trapdoor did not move. He stood there motionless before that shocked assembly of prison governor, chaplain, doctor, assistant sheriff, two warders and hangman.

He was led away at a sign from the governor. Berry adjusted the trapdoor and again pulled the lever. The sides of the drop fell open.

Hurriedly Lee was brought back and placed with toes upon the chalk marks. Again the lever was pulled; again there was no movement of the trap; and again Lee was taken back to his cell. The warders stamped with their heavy boots upon the platform. Berry pulled the lever, and the yawning pit gaped beneath the open trapdoor.

For the third time Lee stood upon that platform, calm and

unperturbed. For the third time the bolt refused to move when the lever was pulled. Lee was taken back to his cell. The prison Governor telegraphed a frantic message to the Home Secretary, who wired back ordering commutation of the sentence to one of penal servitude for life.

Lee served 23 years in gaol. He came out, married, toured the music halls for a space, then kept a "pub", finally going out to the United States where he died about eleven years ago.

As I have pointed out, Lee did not suffer actual hanging, and I know of no similar case to that of Tom Savage.

Let me add a word or two about the popular idea that a person cannot be *tried* twice for the same crime. Again, there is no law on this point, but there is what is called a doctrine of *autrefois acquit* (meaning "formerly acquitted") which is a plea that a person has been acquitted at a previous hearing on the same charge. It goes back to the days of Magna Carta, and is a defence occasionally heard in our courts to-day.

But one *could* be twice charged with the same murder, and on the second occasion could be found guilty and hanged. It would happen in this way.

A person suspected of murder is arrested and brought before a magistrate or bench of magistrates. All the available evidence for the prosecution is gone into, and at the end, the magistrate (or bench) decide that there is not sufficient evidence to commit the accused for trial. In other words a *prima facie* case has not been made out to the satisfaction of the magistrate. The charge against the accused is dismissed.

But—*he has not been put in peril of his life*. That is to say, the magistrate or bench of magistrates who heard the case had no power to try him. Only one of His Majesty's Judges can preside over a murder trial. And although the accused had been called upon to face a charge of murder in the lower court he had not been tried and acquitted by a jury of his fellow-men.

Let us presume that the police continue their enquiries, and happen upon further evidence of this man's guilt. He could then be haled before the courts again, and, if committed for trial, could be sentenced to death as though he had never been charged before. So it *is* possible for a person to be *charged* twice with the same murder.

But let us get back to the main theme of our story, and examine some of the strange dramas which have ended within the walls of the Old Bailey.

Conscience plays queer tricks, and this was never more strongly illustrated than in the case of Thomas Wynne, who came to trial at the Old Bailey *twenty years after he had committed his crime.*

He was in his early twenties when he first came to London after years at sea. Once in town, he "habituated himself with ill company, especially lewd women, leaving no villainy unperpetrated for the support of himself and them in their extravagances".

His real avocation was housebreaking and he flew high in his ambitions, robbing the royal lodgings at Whitehall Palace in Elizabeth's reign. He was sent to prison, but under the Act of Grace luckily received a pardon. He next got a job as scullion with the Earl of Salisbury, but on receiving a lashing for an attack upon one of the Earl's maid servants, he robbed his master and decamped. He then embarked upon a system of robbery which is much in vogue to-day. He would go to a house, and inform the good lady that her husband had been taken suddenly ill, and was lying in a town some few miles away. The distracted wife would rush off to the town mentioned, only to find that there was no truth in Wynne's story. On her return she would find her home ransacked of every valuable.

Wynne varied his thefts. At times he would go to various inns, disguised in the garb of a porter and, picking up any unattended baggage, walk off with it without hindrance. The modern luggate thief works on similar lines.

An old retired linen-draper and his wife, living in Honey

Lane, Cheapside, London, were his last victims in England. He broke into their home, found a richer haul than he expected —some £2,500 in gold—and, fearful of discovery, cut the throats of the old man and woman.

With his ill-gotten gains he fled to Virginia, then being developed by British colonists, and prospered exceedingly. In the meantime, suspicion had fastened upon an old beggar who had been seen in the vicinity of the house in Honey Lane. Although there was no other evidence than his presence near the scene of the crime, this man was arrested, tried, convicted and hanged before the door of the house where the murder had been committed.

Some twenty years passed by, and the Honey Lane murder was forgotten. Out in Virginia, now the owner of rich plantations, Wynne was seized with a sudden desire to return to his native land. He wanted to look round the old haunts, and then go back to Virginia to be buried in his new homeland. He returned to England that same year.

One day he was in a goldsmith's shop in Cheapside when an uproar began in the street. He went out to see what was happening and found that a man had been apprehended by a catchpole (old-time constable) from whom he had broken away. A crowd was in pursuit crying "Stop him! Stop him!" Wynne was caught up in the crowd, and then, as he heard the cry, suddenly stopped in his tracks, and said, "I am the man."

Surprised, the catchpole said, "What do you mean?"

"I am the man you want for the murder of the linen-draper in Honey Lane twenty years ago," replied Wynne. "A man was wrongfully hanged for my crime."

He was taken to Newgate. The fact that one person had already been hanged for the murder placed no difficulties in the way of the trial of Thomas Wynne, who was convicted and sentenced to death.

He too was hanged before the house where the old couple had been murdered.

His wife died in a madhouse; two of his sons were hanged in Virginia for robbery; his plantations were seized for the Queen's use, "and his posterity were reduced to beggary ever afterwards, and died very miserable".

And well they might!

The next trial with which I have to deal is that of another Thomas—better known as 'Tom' Kelsey, who from infancy was a stubborn and untoward brat. Running away from home at the age of fourteen he launched out on a life of crime, and at the age of sixteen had already been sentenced to death for robbing a Mr Johnson in the Strand. His youth saved him, however, but this escape did not cause him to change his ways. Not long after, he corrupted his young cousin David Hughes, by initiating him into the wiles of a "dip", encouraging him to pick pockets in the courtroom at Kingston Assizes. Unfortunately for David, his skill was insufficient and he was caught red-handed and brought before the court the next day. He was ordered to be hanged on a gibbet within sight of the Bench as a warning to others.

Tom Kelsey continued his life of crime undaunted. Like Wynne, he flew high in his depredations. After having robbed the London lodgings of the Earl of Feversham he broke into the house of Lady Grace Pierpont. Somebody gave him away; he was forced to flee to Flanders, where he joined the army. Even here he managed to combine business with pleasure by getting a good haul of booty from the tent of King William III.

On his return to England he once more engaged in housebreaking activities, and was caught entering a shop in Cheapside. Committed to Newgate, he awaited trial at the Old Bailey, in what was known as Common Side.

The Common Side of the gaol was reserved for those who could not afford to pay gaolers' fees for the little additional comforts, which could be obtained on what was called the Master's side of the prison.

There was a debtors' and felons' Common Side of the gaol,

there being a slight difference in the amenities. In the felons' side were five wards; one an underground dungeon called the Stone Hold. A writer known as "B. L. of Twickenham", who was a prisoner in Newgate early in the 18th century, described the Stone Hold as "a terrible stinking, dark and dismal place, situate underground, into which no daylight can come. It was paved with stone; the prisoners had no beds and lay on the pavement whereby they endured great misery."

I mention this by way of mitigation of Tom Kelsey's subsequent behaviour. The only gleam of silver lining to these cloudy surroundings were the tap-room or cellar, where as much strong drink could be obtained as one required, at very cheap rates. Beer was fourpence a quart, wine two shillings a bottle, and brandy fourpence a quartern.

Of the tap-room "B. L." writes:

"It is a great pity that greater decorum is not maintained among the prisoners of the Common Side, especially in the tap-house, for there, by connivance, the felons are permitted to converse and drink with the debtors; by which means such wretchedness abounds therein that the place has the exact aspect of hell itself, and by this means it is to be questioned whether one debtor in ten who enters therein an honest man comes out the same, the wickedness of the place is so great."

It was to the tap-room that Kelsey resorted to drown his sorrows. It was there, too, that a Mr Goodman, one of the turnkeys of the gaol, also resorted to quench his thirst.

What sort of argument ensued—there being no cup ties or Test matches in those days to arouse a natural ire—I know not; but Kelsey took umbrage about something, and having obtained possession of a knife, stabbed the turnkey to death.

Kelsey was brought to the dock of the Old Bailey on a charge of murder instead of the less heinous crime of house-breaking; and, having been sentenced to death, attained the distinction of being executed on a special gallows erected in Newgate Street.

CHAPTER SEVEN

VIRTUE AND VILLAINY

I HAVE already referred to the "packing" of juries, and the pains and penalties they were likely to encounter if they did not find a verdict in accordance with the desire of the judge and sheriffs, but there were some juries whose conscience would not be stifled, and who brought in verdicts according to evidence.

It is pleasing to know that such steadfast adherence to principles has, in one outstanding case, been immortalised. On a wall of one of the lower rooms of the present Old Bailey—a room which was partially wrecked during the Second World War—is a white marble tablet with a black marble surround. On it are inscribed the following words.

> Near this site,
> William Penn and William Mead
> were tried in 1670 for preaching to an unlawful assembly in Grace Church Street. This tablet commemorates the courage and endurance of the jury Thos Vere, Edward Bushell and ten others who refused to give a verdict against them, although locked up without food for two nights, and were fined for their final verdict of Not Guilty.

The trial of William Penn, Quaker and founder of the State of Pennsylvania, is another of those travesties of justice which darkened the 17th century. Penn was the son of wealthy Admiral Penn, who was about to be raised to the peerage when his son announced that he had been converted to the despised new religion. Very soon he became a leader of the Quakers.

As fearless as he was eloquent, he displayed a serene confidence as he stood beside Mead, another Quaker, in the dock at the Old Bailey, and listened to the reading of the indictment.

They were charged with "unlawfully and tumultuously" assembling and addressing the people gathered there in Gracechurch Street, "whereby a great concourse and tumult was made, and continued to the terror and disturbance of His Majesty's subjects".

When they entered the court, someone had removed the prisoners' hats. No sooner were they in the dock, however, than an officer ordered them to put their hats on again. At once the Recorder stormed at them, demanding to know if they realised that they were in the King's Court, and why did they not remove their hats and show the respect they ought to show to the Court.

"I know it to be a Court," replied Penn quietly, "and I suppose it is the King's. But I do not think that pulling off our hats shows any respect."

"Forty marks apiece for contempt," roared the Recorder. Penn shrugged his shoulders. "We came in with our hats off," he said, "and the Court ordered us to put them on, and therefore the Bench ought to be fined rather than Mead and myself."

This was but the first of many scenes in court during the four days the trial lasted. When the Recorder asked Mead if in fact he was present at the meeting, the latter at once replied:

"It is a maxim of your law, *Nemo Tentur seipsum accusare*. Why dost thou endeavour to ensnare me? Is this like a Judge who ought to be of counsel for the prisoner?"

The maxim of law he referred to is that which to-day is sedulously acted upon—that an accused person need not answer any question which is likely to incriminate him.

Penn added, "We declare to all the world we believe it to be our indispensable duty to meet incessantly upon so good an account. Nor shall all the powers on earth divert us from adoring our God who made us."

"You are not brought here for worshipping God, but for breaking the law," tartly responded the Recorder; but Penn was not to be browbeaten, and demanded to know on *what* law the indictment was founded. For that remark he was put in the bail-dock, a little room where prisoners were kept, pending their appearance in the dock.

Mead then took up the challenge, and quoted Sir Edward Coke (the famous lawyer) that "a riot is where three or more are met together to beat a man, to enter forcibly into his land, or to cut down his grass, wood or pales . . ."

"Or to do any other unlawful Act," the Recorder added, then, pulling off his hat with a sardonic bow, he went on, "Thank you, Mr Mead, for telling me what the law is."

"Thee may'st put on thy hat. I have never a fee for thee now," retorted Mead, referring to the fact that the Recorder had, when at the Bar, been employed by him.

The Lord Mayor apparently thought it time to intervene, and remarked, "You profess yourself a meek man, but deserve to have your tongue cut out for affronting the Court."

Still Mead went on, "continuing to revile and reproach the judges", until he too was sent to the bail-dock while the Recorder proceeded to sum up.

This by no means suited Penn, who shouted from the bail-dock that it was illegal to direct the jury in their absence. The Recorder shouted back, however, "You are present, and you *do* hear," and went on to tell the jury what they were to do.

This jury was, however, different from most. After a short retirement they came back with a subtle but indeterminate verdict. It was written down on paper and signed by all the jurors.

"We the jurors hereafter named," it read, "do find William Penn to be guilty of speaking or preaching to an assembly met together in Grace Church Street, the 14th August last 1670. And that William Mead is Not Guilty of the said indictment."

But the Court was not satisfied. The Lord Mayor addressed the jury.

"You have heard that he preached, that he thereby created a

tumult, and that Mead abetted him; they not only disobeyed the martial, but the civil power."

To which Penn made answer, "*We* did not make the tumult, it was they interrupted us. We were by force of arms kept out of our lawful house and met together in a peaceable manner as near to it as the soldiers would give us leave."

And now perceive what happened! An officer of the Court was sworn to keep the jury locked up "without meat, drink, fire or candle until the next morning".

This was done, but when they entered the Court the next day the jury returned exactly the same verdict.

The Recorder stormed and raged.

"I *will* have a positive verdict, or you shall starve for it," he threatened them, and Penn interjected: "They have found William Mead not guilty, and that is a verdict."

"You are indicted for conspiracy," the Recorder countered, "and one being found Not Guilty and not the other, it cannot be a verdict."

William Penn was equal to the occasion, and retorted, "The consent of the jury *is* a verdict; and if William Mead be not guilty, I am acquitted of course. I could not conspire alone."

So the jury were once more sent back to be held yet another night without "meat, drink, fire or candle", and on the morrow, when they again refused to return any other verdict than that already given, they were fined forty marks apiece, and committed to Newgate until their fines should be paid, "for going contrary to plain evidence".

Penn and Mead were also committed to Newgate till their fines for contempt were paid.

From the saintliness of William Penn to the villainy of "Ma" Brownrigg is a long jump. But, as it is a contrast between virtue and villainy, it may profit us to consider the two trials one after another.

In the year 1767 "Old Mother Brownrigg", whose name became a term of execration for those guilty of barbaric cruelty, was arrested and brought to trial at the Old Bailey for the murder of a young girl who had been given into her care.

Elizabeth Brownrigg was the mother of sixteen children herself, and one might have expected that she would possess at least some spark of feeling for the orphan children of others. Not a bit of it. There was no pity in her heart; nor, in spite of her experience as a mother, any sort of sympathy for the women whom she attended in childbirth as the official midwife to the Parish of St Dunstan's.

At the time when this story opens, she was living with her husband and some members of her family in Fleur de Lys Court, Fleet Street. Here she ran a sort of nursing home for maternity cases and offered to take in parish apprentices to teach them the duties of household service. Among her first charges were two girls, Mary Mitchell and Mary Jones.

It was a sad day for these two orphans when they were handed over to this sadistic old harridan by the Parish officers. She took a fiendish delight in flogging them for the most trifling faults.

Mary Jones managed to escape, and on returning to the Foundling Hospital from whence she had been taken, told her sorry story. The Governors of the institution wrote demanding an explanation of the girl's charges, but for some reason the matter was dropped.

Meanwhile, Brownrigg had obtained another girl, Mary Clifford, in place of Mary Jones; and she together with the unfortunate girl Mitchell, suffered terrible beatings and the cruellest treatment. They were flogged with hand broom, cane, horsewhip or any weapon that came to hand. They were beaten until they were senseless, and their mistress speechless with exhaustion.

Mary Clifford, for seeking food when she was nearly starving, was turned out almost naked into a cold yard, and held fast to a door by a jack-chain round her neck, so tight that it threatened to strangle her.

Mary Clifford's step-mother, hearing where the child was to be found, called to see her, but was refused admission. A neighbour, however, warned her that there were terrible doings in the Brownrigg establishment, and Mrs Clifford reported her misgivings to the overseers.

They called upon Mrs Brownrigg and asked that Mary Clifford should be handed over to them, but she said the girl had escaped, and only yielded up Mary Mitchell, who was in such a terrible condition that she was immediately taken to hospital.

There, Mitchell told the authorities that Mary Clifford was still in the house in spite of what Mrs Brownrigg had said. A further search revealed the child locked in a cupboard under a recess in the dining-room. She was in a ghastly condition, her body raw with the violence of her beatings, her wounds showing signs of mortification. Although she was rushed to hospital, the unhappy girl died.

At once there was an outcry, and Mrs Brownrigg with her husband and eldest son appeared in the dock at the Old Bailey charged with the murder of Mary Clifford.

It was a terrible story unfolded in that drab and dingy court by two surviving victims of "Old Mother Brownrigg".

Jones described how she had been stripped and laid across two chairs while Mrs Brownrigg flailed her emaciated body with a whip. When the girl fainted and a bucket of cold water flung over her lacerated form failed to revive her, Mrs Brownrigg had pushed her head into the pail and ducked it in and out.

At times, one or other of the girls had been suspended by her hands from a hook in the ceiling, while her naked body was beaten with broom, whip or cane. Mary Clifford had had no other sleeping place than a cellar under the stairs where coal was usually kept. Into this dark and insanitary hole were flung sacks by way of mattress and covering.

When Mrs Brownrigg went out she left her son in charge, and he also used to strip the girls and lash them with all his strength. Once, when one of the girls blurted out her woes to a woman patient in this "maternity home", Mrs Brownrigg rushed at her and cut her tongue in two places with a pair of scissors.

For some reason which I have not been able to fathom, only the woman was found guilty when they appeared at the Old Bailey, husband and son were acquitted.

On the morning of Brownrigg's execution—after she had been nearly torn to pieces by the howling mob which followed her to Tyburn—the two men kneeled beside her on the scaffold, weeping and praying. As so often happened with these monsters, when the end drew near she was anxious to make her peace with God, and turned to religion. Calmly she embraced husband and son before she was swung off to death. Immediately afterwards, her body was carried to Surgeons' Hall, where it was "anatomised".

It is recorded that "her skeleton has since been exposed in the niche opposite the first door in the Surgeons' Theatre, that the heinousness of her cruelty may make the more lasting impression in the minds of the spectators".

I turn now from the recital of these sordid and harrowing crimes to the story of another Mary, who, although she, too, perished on the scaffold at Tyburn, was guilty of no more than the theft of a few odd pieces of worked muslin from a shop in Ludgate Hill.

Mary Jones was her name—no relation to the Mary Jones in the Brownrigg case. She was a good wife and mother, nor was there anything base about her previous history. She was happily married, the proud mother of two children, and had sufficient of this world's goods to keep her family happy and well. But her enjoyment of life was short-lived; one day the press-gang rounded up her husband and carried him off as an unwilling recruit for the navy. Mary found herself in sore straits, having to fend for her two infants.

The furniture of her home went to buy food for them; they

had no bed on which to lie, and on a cold October day in 1771, with her children ill-clad against the weather, Mary fell to temptation and stole.

Had she been a regular thief she might have escaped detection. But Mary was unlucky. She was caught, and appeared before judges and jury at the Old Bailey. She did not try to mislead the jury, but told them the plain facts of her crime.

"I have been a very honest woman in my lifetime," she told the Court in a quiet, proud voice. "I have two children, and I have worked hard to maintain them since my husband was pressed."

Doubtless a woman of less sterling character, with all Mary's beauty and attraction, could have found a means of living comfortably at the cost of her honour, but Mary was honest and loyal to her husband whom, so far as she knew, she might never see again.

The jury found her Guilty. There was no recommendation to mercy, nor any sign of that quality in the heart of the Recorder who sentenced her to death.

It seems extraordinary that the jury could have remained unmoved by the story of Mary Jones and that the two judges who presided at her trial failed to exercise their discretion by awarding an adequate sentence without sending this young mother to her doom.

Small wonder that, in the frenzy of agony which seized her as she realised that she was to be torn from her children, Mary gave vent to her feelings and cursed both jury and judges as a lot of "old fogrums".

Her neighbours, from Red Lion Street, Whitechapel, signed a petition beseeching the authorities to grant her a reprieve so that she should not be parted from her two babes. But no. She had behaved with "indecency". Had called the court "old fogrums", so she must die at Tyburn.

When she entered the cart for her last earthly journey she carried her youngest child at her breast. The other poor mite was handed over to the authorities. In spite of these harrowing circumstances, circumstances which might well have daunted the stoutest heart, it is recorded that Mary Jones met her death with amazing fortitude.

What happened to her husband? What happened to her children? I do not know. History is mute on those issues. But the story of Mary Jones is not quite finished. Her name has echoed down the years.

Some time after her death, one who has gone down in the annals of crime as "John the Painter", achieved notoriety through being hanged on a gallows *sixty feet high.* The height of the gallows was to emphasise the heinousness of his crime, which was that of setting fire to the rope-house at Portsmouth Dockyard.

We may span the centuries at this point and come to the year 1948 and the debates in both Houses of Parliament on the recent Criminal Justice Bill. There, it will be remembered, on a free vote in the Commons, the death penalty was abolished for a period of five years. There were one or two exceptions. Among these exceptions was that of setting fire to dockyards. And the clause containing this provision is still retained in the Bill in its amended form which came into force at the beginning of 1949.

At the time of the "John the Painter" case, there was no death penalty for arson in a dockyard, and his execution not only set a precedent, but also provided an opportunity for the government of that day to introduce a Bill into Parliament adding yet one more crime to the already long list (some 200) which carried capital punishment.

The case of "John the Painter" is the case upon which is based the clause in the recent Bill retaining the death penalty for the offence.

There were reformers opposed to capital punishment in those days, just as there are to-day. And, when the Bill placing this new offence on the 18th century Statute Book was being debated in Parliament, there was no louder voice in opposition to the Bill or in denouncing the vicious brutality of the penal laws, than that of Sir William Meredith.

As an example he cited the case of Mary Jones, and his voice trembled with emotion as he declared, "I do not believe that a fouler murder was ever committed against law, than the murder of this woman by law."

So, in 1777, from the shadow of the gallows at Tyburn arose the wraith of Mary Jones to appear in the House of Commons through the lips of Sir William Meredith. And nearly two hundred years later, in the present House of Commons, abolitionists of our time as hotly argued for and against the death penalty.

All the women who found their way to Tyburn were not, of course, of the same gentle character as Mary Jones. Barbara Spencer, for example, was one of those wayward young "good time" girls, ever dissatisfied in their humble walk of life, and always yearning for excitement, romance, adventure, but mostly money or the things money could buy.

Her widowed mother, finding her unmanageable, sent her as apprentice to a friendly mantle-maker, who tried to win Barbara from her waywardness by extreme kindness. For a time the girl seemed to respond, but there came a night when she told her mother that she was going to be up early the next morning as she wanted to go to Tyburn to witness a hanging.

Her mother decided that such sights were not good for her seventeen-years-old daughter, and took away Barbara's clothes after the girl had gone to sleep, bolting the bedroom door from the outside to prevent her going.

This only inflamed the girl into rebellion. When her shouts of fury failed to get any response, she leapt from her bedroom window clad only in a shift, and made her way to the home of the girl friend with whom she was to attend the executions.

This girl lived at a house near St Giles Pound, a none too salubrious neighbourhood, inhabited by thieves and vagabonds of all types. Here Barbara was introduced to a gang of coiners, who held out the lure of easy money if she would engage in passing counterfeit coins.

The idea appealed to her, and for a time she was successful. Of course, she was caught eventually, but in view of her youth was only fined and imprisoned. Even so, she failed to learn her lesson, for when she was released, she started coining on her own account.

Once more she found her way into the dock at the Old Bailey, and this time her youth did not avail her. She was sentenced to be strangled and burnt to death.

A very unruly prisoner, she created terrible scenes in the condemned hold. The news of her exploits spread abroad outside the prison and in consequence a larger crowd than usual gathered at Tyburn, gleefully anticipating a "good show", but they were disappointed. When, amid their jeers and jibes and ribald jests, she was tied to the stake, she became very devout. Her disappointed audience pelted her with stones and refuse in an attempt to jolly her into providing them with better entertainment, but Barbara kept her head bowed in prayer.

Let me hark back on my story for a moment to mention briefly the first recorded hanging in the Old Bailey. Tyburn ceased to be the recognised place of execution in 1783, and the spot at Newgate end of the street of Old Bailey became the official rendezvous for the condemned. But nearly a century before this change, there had been a hanging at Newgate, when "Nan" Hereford was executed in the year 1698.

"Nan"—her real name was Ann—was a clever thief, whose adeptness at this form of crime was only equalled by her prowess as a pugilist. She would fight any man at any weight, and was one of the earliest male impersonators in our history. She would sally forth dressed in men's clothes the better to carry out her thieving exploits. She looked the part, too, and her disguise saved her from detection on many occasions. If it had not been for her betrayal by a woman rival she might have escaped altogether. As it was, she was arrested, flung into Newgate, and promptly began to make the lives of prisoners and officers alike a hell upon earth. Irons or shackles could not restrain her, and the climax came when she set fire to the gaol. When, finally, she stood in the dock, she was charged with arson in addition to her other crimes.

It was considered fitting that, instead of being taken to Tyburn, Nan should be hanged outside Newgate, the scene of her crime. She thus achieved the distinction of being the first malefactor to be hanged in the Old Bailey.

CHAPTER EIGHT

CHAPLAINS AS GALLOWS BIRDS

LET us leave trials for the time being, and return to conditions in Newgate. In 1750, there occurred an outbreak of fever so virulent that two judges, the Lord Mayor of London, and Aldermen, several of the jury and a number of spectators who had attended the trials at the Old Bailey were stricken down and died.

For years, prisoners had been dying in great numbers through the insanitary conditions in Newgate, and little notice was taken, but when two of His Majesty's judges and several important men were struck down, something had to be done about it.

It was found that the infection had been carried into the court-room of the Old Bailey from the prison cells beneath the building, and a huge windmill ventilator was built on top of one of the towers of the gateway to carry off the infectious atmosphere. The installation of this Heath Robinson-like contraption caused great alarm in the neighbourhood, for the residents there complained most strongly that the poisonous air drawn from the germ-laden cells would most likely kill them. Nor was it entirely effective, for in 1772 there was another outbreak of gaol fever which laid low a number of officers of the court.

In the meantime there had been introduced a custom which holds fast to this day, a custom as pretty as it is quaint. Anyone present in the Old Bailey Courts to-day may be surprised to see the learned judges, Recorder, or Common Serjeant carrying a nosegay of flowers with them to their places on the Bench.

This is a survival of the custom to which I have referred as having been introduced after the outbreak of gaol fever in 1750. The stench from the felons' cells was so fearsome, and the risk of contagion so great, that a bunch of sweet-smelling herbs was always carried by the judges and all in attendance upon them on the Bench, while other herbs were strewn about the dock, together with strong vinegars as a sort of disinfectant.

You can guess the kind of place Newgate must have been. The whole gaol with the exception of the Press Yard—the best part of the gaol, consisting of a number of rooms around an open Yard, for which the wealthy and the favoured few paid varying sums for the additional luxury of living there—was a dank, dark, miserable place with only a glimmer of illumination here and there. The air was foul through overcrowding and lack of sanitation.

In *The London Chronicle* (1750) there is mentioned "a new scheme for enlarging the prison of Newgate by knocking down back-houses near the Sessions House yard. It is intended to erect Piazzas so that the prisoners may have room to walk about in the open air." But nothing was done at that time, although there were everlasting rumours of re-building and improvements that were to be carried out. In 1764, for example, *The London Chronicle* stated that in the new plan for re-building the prison, "there is to be a sort of square where there will be continual running water for to keep them clean, and a large room with a fire-place to keep them warm. At night, they will be put into different cells or rooms as at Bedlam."

Newgate was in a terrible state of repair at the time of which I write, and the Common Council reported to the City Corporation in 1755 that the prison was "incapable of improvement or tolerable repair", adding that "it is overcrowded with victims of public justice, under the complicated distresses of poverty, nastiness and disease".

In 1767, Sir Stephen Jansen described Newgate as an "abominable sink of beastliness and corruption".

In 1770, by Act of Parliament, the building of a "new and commodious Jail" was begun. This was the last of the Newgate prisons; the same gaol which I saw being demolished in 1902, before the present Old Bailey was built upon its site.

You will remember that when Newgate was badly damaged during the Great Fire of London in 1666, the old Justice or Sessions House was also partially burned, and had to be almost rebuilt. Strype, the historian of that day, said in 1726 that the new court was a "fair and stately building, having galleries at both sides or ends for the reception of spectators".

When Newgate was rebuilt in 1770, the Sessions House was also rebuilt, and I may say from my own brief knowledge of that building, which also existed until the opening of the new Old Bailey in 1907, that it was a stuffy, dingy, and unhygienic building. Its ill-lit, narrow, winding stairs leading up to the court-rooms left one with a brooding sense of unillumined justice.

But again I am leaping ahead of my story, and would return to another Old Bailey trial, which, although of little moment in the history of the court, made legal history.

This was the trial of Thomas Wilford in 1752, and it is of interest to-day, when so much has been written and said on the subject of capital punishment.

As far back as 1701 this controversy had been initiated, with the publication of a pamphlet by one who preferred to remain unknown except for the initials, J. R., M.A. The title of this pamphlet was *Hanging not Punishment enough for Murtherers High-way Men and House-breakers.*

The author argued that if it be right to put to death a man found guilty of stealing goods to the value of five shillings, then "he who puts me in fear of my life and breaks the Kings Peace, and it may be murthers me at last, and burns my house, deserves another sort of Censure; and if the one must die, the other should be made to *feel* himself die".

J. R. therefore suggested that a murderer should be hanged alive in chains, and left to starve, or alternatively he should be broken on the wheel or whipped to death.

A few years later another M.A. published *An Essay humbly offered for an Act of Parliament to put down Capital Crimes and the Loss of many Lives, and to promote a desirable improvement and Blessing in the Nation.*

This was a Mr George Ollyffe who looked upon capital punishment as having very little terror, and argued that "an execution that is attended with more lasting torment, may strike a far greater Awe, much to lessen if not to put a stop to their shameless crimes".

Mr Ollyffe thought that breaking on the wheel was the most suitable means of putting down murder, because "the criminals run through ten thousand thousand of the most exquisite agonies, as there are moments in the several hours and days during the inconceivable torture of their bruised, broken and disjointed limbs to the last period".

You must not adjudge Mr Ollyffe too heartless, however, for he revealed a gentle thought for others. He suggested that the punishment he recommended should be carried out some twenty poles from the usual execution places, so that the cries of the victim should not "disturb the common passengers".

In 1752 Parliament passed an Act "For Better Preventing the horrid Crime of Murder", but they did not adopt any of the above suggestions. After remarking that murder had become more frequent of late, they advocated that "some further Terror and peculiar Mark of Infamy be added to the Punishment of Death". It was directed that persons should be executed the next day but one after having been found Guilty; that the judge may order the prisoner to be hanged in chains (after death) and in every case the body handed over for dissection.

You may wonder why such quick despatch should be thought an extra terror to the doomed person. Most people, I should imagine, would like to get it over and done with, but the reason was that it gave the condemned man no time to repent and so launched him into eternity without hope of Heaven.

It was under this Act that poor Thomas Wilford, a one-armed boy of seventeen, was made to suffer. He was the first person to be sentenced under this Act, and his story is almost as sad as that of Mary Jones.

Thomas was a cripple employed at the workhouse in St Giles-in-the-Field. While working here he met a girl of ill-fame with whom he fell in love. He was seventeen, and the girl was pretty and attractive, and only a year or two older than the boy. A romance quickly began, and they were married at the Fleet one Wednesday. The following Sunday the bride went out with a former lover. She did not return till midnight, and naturally her husband wanted to know where she had been. A toss of her pretty head, and a sharp "in the park" was all the information she would give him.

There were probably other taunting words. We don't know. All that we do know is that Tom lost his temper, seized a knife, and throwing his wife to the ground, knelt on her and nearly severed her head from her body.

Then he got quietly up, and being met by a neighbour blurted out his sorry story.

"I have just murdered my poor wife," he confessed. "She whom I loved as dearly as my own life."

Tom was duly arrested and brought to trial. At the Old Bailey he pleaded Guilty, but the Court refused to accept the plea, and put him back till the last day of the Sessions. Again he pleaded Guilty, and again was put back, until, ultimately, he was persuaded to "put himself on trial", the equivalent of a plea of Not Guilty.

If a plea of provocation was raised, it must have fallen on deaf ears, for the jury brought in a verdict of Guilty, and it is of interest to-day to read a change in the form of the death sentence, as it was then pronounced.

"Thomas Wilford, you stand convicted of the horrid and unnatural crime of murdering Sarah, your wife. This Court doth adjudge that you be taken back to the place from whence

Newgate Chapel in 1809. The "death sermon" is being read to those about to be executed

From a coloured print by Rowlandson, published in 1809

you came, and there fed upon bread and water till Wednesday next when you are to be taken to the common place of execution, and there hanged by the neck until you are dead, after which your body is to be publicly dissected and anatomised . . ."

So Thomas Wilford made history—sad history at that. But before I leave his story, let me point out how, gradually, things were developing.

Not so many years before, prisoners were being taken to the Press Room (not Press Yard) there to be crushed to death for *not* pleading to a charge. Now, every care was being taken to safeguard the prisoner by not accepting a plea of Guilty, even though it had been repeated.

One of the most unhappy men who savoured the misery of Newgate Gaol was Dr Dodd, son of a clergyman, and himself Prebendary of Brecon, Chaplain in Ordinary to George III and Minister of Magdalen Hospital for reclaiming young women who had "swerved from the Path of Virtue".

Dodd was a poet, and compiler of *Beauties of Shakespeare*. Later, finding literature far from lucrative, he renounced it and entered the Church. Here his eloquence attracted the attention of Horace Walpole as well as that of innumerable society beauties. He rivalled many of our highwaymen in the attentions bestowed upon him by the fair sex.

Walpole described his sermons as "flowery" and remarked that they "set all the ladies of fashion sobbing".

Certainly Dodd was a great showman in his time, and ever ready to exploit any opportunity that came his way. For example he wrote many religious works, in which he included the most fulsome and flattering dedications to those whom he sought to impress. In this way he was made Prebendary of Brecon, and King's Chaplain, and with these recommendations was appointed tutor to the Earl of Chesterfield's son.

With always an eye to the main chance the Doctor dabbled in lotteries, and having won a prize of £1,000, he built a chapel near Buckingham Palace and "bought a share" in a chapel in Bloomsbury. Apparently these investments failed to show the return he hoped. He became overwhelmed with debt, and brought out more religious works in the hope of winning patrons by his dedications.

His ambition was great, and when the rich living of St George's, Hanover Square, became vacant, he was misguided enough to write to Lady Apsley, wife of the Lord Chancellor, offering £3,000 for the appointment.

This simply was not done. And for his attempted bribery he was struck off the list of chaplains. Dodd decided to go abroad with Lord Chesterfield until things blew over. At this time he was still in receipt of £800 a year, but this was not enough for the extravagant pastor. He went to a broker named Robertson, and got him to negotiate a loan of £4,200, saying that the Earl of Chesterfield was in need of money, and had engaged him (Dodd) as a go-between, to avoid publicity. Dodd forged the Earl's signature and obtained the loan. The forgery, however, was discovered and he was arrested and brought to trial at the Old Bailey.

He had already repaid much of the money, and had given a judgment on his goods for the remainder. Lord Chesterfield did not want to carry the matter further, but the Lord Mayor compelled the prosecution, and Dodd was found Guilty and sentenced to death.

His case excited the sympathy of Press and public alike. Dr Johnson was to the fore in his efforts to secure a pardon for the erring clergyman. He not only wrote the speech which Dodd made to the jury at his trial, but also wrote several petitions, together with the condemned man's own death sermon, which the Doctor delivered to his fellow-prisoners just before his execution.

Dodd had many friends and Dr Johnson told Boswell that there was £1,000 awaiting any gaoler who could arrange the escape of the one-time King's Chaplain. A scheme was advanced which involved the use of a wax figure of the prisoner, and the model was actually made, but somehow the plot never came off.

Dodd made a sorry figure at his execution. He had been so sure of a reprieve that when it did not come he lapsed into a state of despair and stupidity. His hat flapped around his eyes, which swivelled unseeingly from object to object except when they were momentarily closed in prayer. The hangman, in removing his hat, also removed his wig. With a last vestige of self-respect, Dodd put on a nightcap to hide his scalp. Unfortunately it was too small and only increased his look of foolish dejection. Soon afterwards, apparently absorbed in despair, he was swung from the cart. For a short while he hung there amid the desultory cheers of the crowd who had tired of his lengthy praying, and wanted more action in the last scene.

Many years before his arrest, he had, with almost prophetic vision, written a pamphlet entitled, *The Frequency of Capital Punishment, inconsistent with Justice, Sound Policy and Religion.* And while in Newgate awaiting his doom, he wrote another, *Prison Thoughts*, in which he again dwelt on the subject and prophesied the abolition of the procession to Tyburn and perhaps public execution. He broke into verse on this occasion, the lines running:

> *. . . yes, the day—*
> *I joy in the idea—will arrive*
> *When Britons philanthropic shall reject*
> *The cruel custom, to the sufferer cruel,*
> *Useless and baneful to the gaping crowd.*

When his body was cut down, it was taken at once to the house of the undertaker where a hot bath was waiting. Dr Pott, a very celebrated surgeon of that day, did everything possible to restore life. So great was the crowd which had gathered to watch the execution, however, that there had been more than usual delay in getting the body through their ranks, and all efforts at reviving Dodd were in vain.

It so happened that another clergyman, the Reverend James Hackman, also destined to perish on the scaffold at Tyburn, was present at Dodd's execution.

Hackman was hanged for the murder of a Miss Reay—mistress to the Earl of Sandwich—of whom he had become enamoured, pursuing her over a period of years with an ardour which is revealed in some of the finest love letters ever written. In one of them he mentions Dodd. The letter is dated 27 June 1777, 5 o'clock, and reads:

"As I want both appetite and spirits to touch my dinner though it has been standing before me these ten minutes, I can claim no merit in writing to you . . . Don't be angry, but I have been to see the last of poor Dodd. The scene was affecting—it was the first of the kind I had ever seen; and shall certainly be the last."

Hackman goes on to describe the execution very much as I have done above, adding, "For my own part I detected myself in a certain manner, accompanying his body with the motion of my own . . . How shocking that a man with whom I have eaten and drunk, should leave the world in such a manner . . ."

James Hackman was an officer in the Army before he became a clergyman, and while he was on a recruiting campaign at Huntingdon, he was invited to Hinchinbrooke House, the home of Lord Sandwich. This Lord Sandwich was such an inveterate gambler that he could not bear to leave the gaming-table even for food. Instead he had prepared for him a meal of meat placed between slices of bread. Yes—he was the inventor, originator or what you will, of the Sandwich, which has carried his name ever since.

At Hinchinbrooke, Hackman met Miss Margaret Reay, who for years had lived with the Earl and had borne him several children. The young soldier fell in love at first sight, and from the letters which passed between the pair it would seem that there was also great affection on the part of Miss Reay. There was at the same time, a modest dalliance which bespoke the respect and loyalty she had for Lord Sandwich, who had given her his protection.

One glimpses the reluctance of the lady in a letter written by Hackman in which he begins, "My dearest Margaret,—I will not take advantage of the sweet reluctant, amorous confession which your candour gave me yesterday. If to make me happy, be to make my M. otherwise; then, happiness, I'll have none of thee."

I wish I could reproduce more of the fragrant epistles which both lovers wrote to each other. As Miss Reay said in one of her letters: "I argued the matter stoutly—my head on his Lordship's side, my heart on yours. At last they seemed to say, as if the oath of allegiance, which I had taken to gratitude, at a time when Heaven knows, I had never heard of love, should be void, and I should be at full liberty to devote myself body and soul, to—— But call on me tomorrow before dinner and I'll tell you of their final judgment."

So the secret love affair went on, Hackman giving up his Army career to become vicar of Wiverton, in Norfolk. Letters, impassioned and lyrical, continued to pass between them with the man always urging the woman to marry him; the woman yearning to do so, but held back by love for her children, her gratitude to her noble lover, and—by the fear of the contumely to which Hackman would be held up, by marriage to the Earl's "cast off woman" as she put it.

But Hackman was blind to all except his need for Margaret, who, although still in her early teens when the Earl took her under his protection, was some years older than her lover.

He became obsessed with the notion that Margaret Reay did not love him, otherwise she would come to him, and in this state of mind decided to commit suicide. On the fatal day he wrote a letter to a friend declaring his intention of taking his life. There was no mention of his intention to kill Miss Reay. That night he went to the theatre where he knew his loved one would be—probably to take a last farewell glimpse of her. But the sight of her played such havoc with his feelings that he could not stay in the theatre to see the play through. It was called *Love in a Village*.

He was armed with two pistols and waited outside the theatre, perhaps to impress the woman with the tragedy of his love by shooting himself before her eyes. Whatever may have been in his mind, the fact is that he fired two shots; one at Margaret Reay, who fell mortally wounded, the other at himself, with less tragic results. As he fell at his lady's feet, only slightly wounded, he beat his head with the butt of his pistol and called upon the bystanders to kill him.

Grub Street celebrated the story:

"*A Sandwich favourite was this fair,*
And her he dearly loved;
By whom six children had, we hear;
This story fatal proved.

"*A clergyman, O Wicked one*
In Covent Garden shot her.
No time to cry upon her God,
It's hoped he's not forgot her."

One of the children referred to was Basil Montague, one of the great prison reformers of his day. The founder of the "Society for the Diffusion of Knowledge upon the Punishment of Death", he did much to bring home to the public the barbaric cruelty of our laws. In 1801 so active was he in pursuit of his beliefs that on one occasion he rode all through the night to save the lives of two men, for whom he had obtained a reprieve, and arrived just in time.

Hackman was visited by the great biographer James Boswell in Newgate, where he lay for a few days awaiting death. During this period the condemned man wrote to a friend, "You must suffer me to mention the tenderness and greatness of mind of my dear B."

While in Newgate, he dreamed a dream in which he thought his beloved looked down upon him in his plight, and—smiled.

Hackman wrote to his friend Charles:

"She saw me, where I was steeped to the lips in misery. She saw me; but without a tear, without one sigh . . . She smiled at all my sufferings. Yes, she even enjoyed the tortures, the wracking of my soul . . . Flames and brimstone . . . corporal sufferance—were paradise to such eternal hell as this.

"Oh. How I rejoiced, how I wept, sobbed with joy when I awoke, and discovered it was only a dream and found myself *in the condemned cell of Newgate.*"

Was there ever a more poignant letter penned within those sorry walls?

CHAPTER NINE

REFORMERS *VERSUS* AUTHORITIES

REFORMERS are always with us. They continue tirelessly in their efforts to remove the injustices or grievances of this imperfect world. The fight for better conditions in prison life has gone on through the ages, and is still an issue to-day.

It is impossible within the scope of this book to deal with the whole history of penal reform, but we can give a brief glimpse of the gradual manner in which improvements were brought about.

That there was need for the work of the reformers is obvious from the description already given of conditions in Newgate.

Pepys in his Diary for 1 August, 1667, wrote:

"Sir Richard Ford the Recorder (of the Old Bailey) says that the keeper of Newgate hath at this day made his house the only nursery of rogues, prostitutes, pick-pockets and thieves in the world, where they were held and entertained and the whole society met; and that for the sake of the Sheriffs they durst not this day commit him, for fear of making him let out the prisoners, but are fain to go by artifices to deal with him."

And you will recall the merry little racket of "fees" charged for all manner of privileges, in which the governor, keeper and even prisoners themselves shared the financial benefits.

In the year 1400 a charter was granted by Henry III allowing the sheriff only *one* perquisite of fourpence from each person as he or she was liberated from the gaol. This privilege was retained until 1732, when it was ordered that prisoners should be released without fee. The order was evaded for many years, and in 1774 it was considered necessary to pass an Act by which prisoners, found Not Guilty, were released in open court.

In 1771 another reform was introduced. Before then, all prisoners, as I have already mentioned, entered the dock for trial laden with handcuffs and leg irons. It did not matter what the charge against them might be, murder or petty theft; they all appeared before judge and jury chained and manacled as though they were dangerous criminals.

The rank injustice of this indignity caused John Wilkes, one of the City Sheriffs, to demand the removal of this open branding of an accused person before he or she had been tried. He gained overwhelming support, and an order was made that no prisoner should appear in court with irons on the day of the trial.

This brought about an agitation for a further reform. An inquiry was held at which it was urged that to fetter unconvicted prisoners, who might thus be shackled for weeks or even months while awaiting trial, was an outrage. The prison officers, ever jealous of their powers, insisted that if prisoners were unfettered, not even Newgate could hold their charges; higher walls would have to be built at great expense to keep them in, they declared. And, they naïvely added, it would be impossible to distinguish prisoners from visitors without this means of identification.

Their plea was so successful that another half-century passed before prisoners were allowed to go about their prison tasks unshackled.

One of the famous visitors who did much to alleviate the mental anguish of prisoners in Newgate, was one Silas Told, a Wesleyan minister, whose heart was touched by the stories of suffering he had heard.

Ten felons under sentence of death were the first to come under his influence, and the success of his teaching was made evident on the day of their execution. On the way to Tyburn one of the ten, a man named Lancaster, exhorted the ribald throng to "come to the Throne of Grace", assuring them that they would find a merciful God, just as he had done.

A strange thing happened after Lancaster had been hanged. There was nobody to claim his body, and the surgeon's mob—ever in attendance for just such a chance to snatch the body for cutting up—whisked it off to Paddington. Eight sailors, who had turned up late for the entertainment, found out what had happened, and went off in search of Lancaster's body.

Let me give the rest of the story as related by Silas Told.

"When the sailors had obtained the body, two of them cast it on their shoulders and carried him round by Islington. They being tired, two others laid themselves under the weight of the body and carried it thence to Shoreditch. Then two more carried it from Shoreditch to Coverley's Fields. At length after they were all rendered weary, and unable to carry it further . . . there was unanimous assent to lay it on the first doorstep they came to. They did so and went their way! This gave birth to a great riot in the neighbourhood which brought an old woman downstairs. When she saw the corpse lie at the step of the door she proclaimed with an agitated spirit, 'Lord here is my son John Lancaster'."

It is emphasised that the sailors "had no knowledge of the body, nor to whom he belonged when living".

Silas Told did some wonderful work in Newgate. The felons swore and cursed at the preacher, yet he managed to found a congregation of some forty debtors who regularly attended his services.

Two other names outstanding in the history of penal reform are those of John Howard and Elizabeth Fry.

John Howard, the son of a London merchant, lived a secluded but philanthropic life as a country squire in Bedfordshire until the year 1773. Then, at the age of 47, he was made High Sheriff of Bedford, and in this capacity visited Bedford Prison. The conditions angered and horrified him so much that he immediately resolved to do what he could to remedy the many abuses.

It was he who campaigned against the system by which keepers of gaols throughout the country, together with their subordinates, were unsalaried, and depended for their livelihood upon the fees they extracted from the prisoners themselves.

He came to London and saw the Newgate Gaol then in process of construction, and commented that "without more than ordinary care the prisoners in it will be in great danger of gaol fever".

In 1778 the new prison was completed and opened, and in 1779 Howard visited Newgate again and gave a more or less favourable account. Writing in 1784, he stated: "At my visit in 1779 the gaol was clean and free from offensive scents. On the felons' side there were only three sick in one of the upper wards . . . Of the 141 felons, there were 91 convicts and fines who had only the prison allowance of a penny loaf a day. Mr Akerman generously contributed towards their relief. In the felons' court the table of fees, painted on a board was hung up."

Mr Akerman, it should be mentioned, was an enlightened and kindly keeper of Newgate who, in 1770, appeared before a Committee of the House of Commons, where he described Newgate as "a sink of filth and den of iniquity". He declared it to be over-crowded, ill-disciplined, badly ventilated and ill-supplied with water. His endeavours to palliate the lot of his prisoners is one of the brighter spots in the history of Newgate. His conduct, too, at the subsequent Gordon riots of 1780 was courageous in the extreme.

The riots arose out of the conflict between Protestant and Catholic which raged so wildly about this time. Young Lord George Gordon, third son of the Duke of Gordon and a fervent Protestant, became President of the Protestant Association which was formed to secure a repeal of an Act of William III removing some of the disabilities suffered by the Catholics.

In June, 1780, Lord George marched at the head of 60,000 supporters to the House of Commons where he presented a petition. Unfortunately, among the crowd were well over a thousand criminals who, seeing a chance of loot and plunder, seized the opportunity to incite the throng into violent disorder. Many Roman Catholic places of worship were damaged and robbed.

Two days later even more violent riots took place, and it was on this occasion that the Bank of England and other public buildings were attacked, and the prisons forced.

Lord George Gordon was arrested, brought to trial, and acquitted as insane. Twenty-one of his henchmen were not so lucky. They were found Guilty and executed. It was ironic justice in a way, for they were tried at the Old Bailey which they had nearly destroyed, and awaited their doom in that part of Newgate Gaol which they had failed to damage.

For a vivid description of the scenes of disorder which obtained when the rioters attacked the gaol, there is no need to go further than the Old Bailey Sessions Papers for June of that year.

On the evening of June 6 just after six o'clock, the mob came surging down Holborn into the Old Bailey. Three flags bearing Protestant mottoes were carried in front.

Exactly at seven, one of the ringleaders knocked on the door of the keeper's quarters. But Mr Akerman had already heard the rioters were marching on Newgate, and had taken the precaution of barricading the door with furniture.

Receiving no answer to his knock, the ringleader bowed to the waiting crowd and then pointed to the door. Thirty men walking abreast and armed with crowbars, mattocks and chisels strode forward, followed by an "innumerable company" carrying bludgeons and the spokes of cart wheels. The rioters attacked the various doors—debtors' and felons', and that of Mr Akerman.

Mr Akerman's quarters were the first to be breached, the windows being smashed in with a scaffold pole carried by the mad Quaker son of a rich corn merchant. A lad then climbed on to his shoulders and smashed in the shutters by furious blows with his head! Eventually the house was entered, pictures and furniture being hurled into the street and set ablaze.

Attention was then turned to the gate of the prison itself. The mob rushed on it with sledge-hammers and pickaxes which they had stolen from coachmakers and blacksmiths in Drury Lane. To speed their efforts, they piled blazing furniture from the Akerman home against the gate, to set it on fire. The turnkeys inside countered by pushing the burning furniture away with broomsticks poked through the hatch, and swilling the fire with water. But all in vain; gradually the fire and the persistent battering breached the remaining doors, and the rioters had free access to the prison.

George Crabbe, the poet, had only recently arrived in London at this time, and lived in humble lodgings over a barber's shop near the Exchange. He went for a walk on the day of the riots and reached Ludgate Hill just as the rioters swarmed into the Old Bailey. He later described how he saw some of the prisoners coming up out of their dingy cells bowed down with their heavy irons, looking pale and scared. Some of them were carried off in triumph, on horseback, their irons clanking as they rode away to freedom.

Mentioning that he saw Akerman with four rioters in custody, whose release the mob was demanding, Crabbe says, "How he escaped or where he has gone I know not . . . As I was standing near the spot, another body of men approached—I suppose five hundred—and Lord George Gordon in a coach drawn by the mob towards Alderman Bull's bowing as he passed. He is a lively looking young man in appearance, but nothing more, although just now he is the reigning hero . . . The prison was a remarkably strong building; but determined to force it, they broke the gates with crow-bars and climbed up the outside of the cell part . . . they broke the roof, tore away the rafters and having got ladders, descended. Not Orpheus himself had more courage or better luck. Flames all around them, and a body of soldiers expected, they defied and laughed at all opposition.

"The prisoners escaped. I stood and saw about twelve women and eight men ascend from their confinement to the open air, and they were conducted through the streets in their chains. Three of these were to be hanged on Friday . . . Newgate was at this time open to all. Anyone might get in, and, what was never the case before, any one might get out . . . But I must not omit what struck me most; about twelve of the mob getting to the top of the debtor's prison while it was burning, to halloo, they appeared rolled in black smoke mixed with sudden bursts of fire—like Milton's infernals, who were as familiar with flame as with each other."

The next day, one might have seen the burly, carelessly-dressed figure of Dr Johnson making his way to the scene of the conflagration.

"On Wednesday," he wrote, "I walked with Dr Scott to look at Newgate and found it in ruins, with the fire yet glowing. As I went by, the Protestants were plundering the Sessions House at the Old Bailey. There were not I believe a hundred; but they did their work at leisure, in full security, without sentinels, without trepidation, as men lawfully employed in full day."

Of course Newgate was not the only place attacked by the rioters. They burned the Catholic Chapel in Lincoln's Inn Fields, gutted the house of Sir George Saville in Leicester Square, burnt the Fleet and the King's Bench prisons and attacked the Bank of England.

But not even the raging fires which were lit that night could destroy the heavy stone walls of the recently built Newgate Gaol, although it became necessary to carry out extensive rebuilding operations. The same plan was retained, and in due course prisoners were again housed in the sinister-looking building which stood at the corner of Newgate Street.

Conditions inside were not very much improved, in spite of the fact that John Howard had already begun to awaken the public conscience to the abuses which marked prison life and darkened the administration of our law.

In the meantime, there had been one small advance in the way of reform. The unholy processions from Newgate to Tyburn, of those unhappy souls doomed to perish at the hands of the hangman, were stopped. For some 600 years these processions had been a feature of our city life, and there is no question of their popularity, but on the morning of November 7, 1783, the last hanging at Tyburn took place. The hero of this drama was John Austin, who had been convicted at the Old Bailey of robbing John Spicer "and cutting and wounding him in a cruel manner".

Let us spare a few lines to describe the end of Austin who, though he "behaved with great composure" on the last of these historic journeys to Tyburn, "trembled greatly" while the noose was being adjusted. The Ordinary having done his duty, John made his closing speech as follows:

"Good people, I request your prayers for the salvation of my departing soul; let my example teach you to shun the bad ways I have followed; keep good company, and mind the word of God."

As the cart was drawn away, the halter slipped to the back of his neck, and in consequence it was some time before he died. Thus was the curtain rung down on Tyburn, and on the life of John Austin, together.

The new rendezvous for public hanging was that spot in the roadway of Old Bailey, just outside the present main entrance to the court-house. At that time it was the Debtors' Door of Newgate Gaol.

Lest it be thought that the transfer of executions from Tyburn to Newgate was due to any humanitarian scruples—such as shortening the journey for the doomed—let me hasten to explain that the change was made for other reasons. The homes of the "quality" were beginning to spread out from the City confines towards Tyburn; and the occupants were anxious that their seclusion and exclusiveness should not be trespassed upon by hordes of drunken revellers embarked on their all-night wait for the morning's execution, nor their sight offended by the spectacle of gibbets on their doorstep.

There were those who decried the shifting of the scene, so to speak; among them none other than the redoubtable Dr Johnson, who complained:

"The age is running mad after innovation. All the business of the world is to be done in a new way. Tyburn itself is not safe from the fury of innovation. No, Sir! It is not an improvement; they object that the old method drew together a number of spectators. Sir, executions are intended to draw spectators. If they do not draw spectators, they don't answer their purposes. The old method was most satisfactory to all parties; the public was gratified by a procession; the criminal was supported by it. Why is all this to be swept away?"

On December 9 of that same year (1783) the street of Old Bailey became the official place of execution. To celebrate the occasion there was introduced the new "drop", and the gallows was built with three crossbeams to accommodate as many rows of victims. The drop was an ingenious device which did away with the necessity of a cart.

Previously, as you will have gathered, there was no mechanised drop; the doomed person stood either on a cart, which at the appropriate moment was driven away, or else was compelled to mount a ladder, from which he was turned off by the hangman giving the ladder a twist.

The new drop was a more certain process. A large hinged trap-door was let into the platform of the scaffold upon which the prisoner or prisoners stood beneath their respective crossbeams, arms pinioned behind them, and noose arranged about their necks with the knot in just the right position—under, and slightly behind, the left ear.

The loose edge of the platform was held by a stout pin which, on being withdrawn, allowed the trap-door to fall

Preparing for an execution

From a print in the British Museum

inwards, plunging its human burden into the pit below.

We have progressed even further in our mechanics since then, and to-day we have a double trap-door opening in the middle and secured by two well-greased and polished bolts which are withdrawn by the pull of a lever.

The doomed person stands with toes touching a chalk-marked line. The hangman pulls the lever, the two trap-doors open inwards, and the victim vanishes from sight.

During the last year of Tyburn as a place of execution, 108 malefactors were condemned to death at the Old Bailey, 58 of these were sentenced in one Sessions—the September Sessions—for stealing, and the Deputy Recorder of that day remarked that it was painful and alarming "to behold a bar so crowded with persons whose wickedness and imprudence had induced them to commit such enormous crimes as the laws of their country justly and necessarily punish with death. *Those laws, while they are founded in equity and executed with lenity, impartiality, and rectitude, are written in blood.*"

The italics are mine, for not a few of the culprits whom he thus addressed were men and women who had stolen to save their children from starvation.

In the December Sessions of the same year (1783) twenty-four were sentenced to death and ninety were transported for *first offences.*

On December 9 the first hangings at the new gallows took place in front of Newgate. Ten unhappy felons met their death in a bunch, the usual morbid crowd looking on with fascinated eyes at this sorry spectacle.

It would seem that the year 1783 was fraught with conflicting influences; for, while there were attempts to ameliorate the lot of prisoners, there was a sudden outbreak of crime which caused the Secretary of State to advise the King that judges should be ordered to apply the law at its fullest and harshest.

The cause of the "crime wave", as we should call it to-day, was probably due to the discharge from the army of thousands of soldiers (after the War of Independence in America) who, penniless and starving, took to thieving and robbery with violence.

Newgate, together with other prisons up and down the land, became as crowded as ever, and His Majesty's Judges awarded death, transportation and other punishments with a lavish hand.

In the year 1785, forty-nine persons occupied the condemned hold in Newgate at one time. In addition, other parts of the gaol were occupied by hundreds awaiting transportation. On February 2, 1785, twenty men were hanged in a batch outside the debtors' door. Five of them were hanged for assaulting a man and robbing him of two glass drops set in metal, valued at 3d; a one-inch rule, value 2d; two papers of nails, value 1d; two shillings and a counterfeit half-penny.

Such was the state of crime and punishment up to the 19th century, and so it continued, as we shall see, well into the Victorian era.

The reformers were still active, and very early in the 19th century managed to impress upon the minds of the authorities that, in spite of the ferocity of sentences, there had been no diminution of crime; and they urged that a little leniency towards lesser crimes might reduce the number of more serious offences. They pointed out that if a man knew he would be hanged for stealing twopence, then he might well think that a hold-up, or even a murder with a larger amount as booty, would be worth while.

The authorities were apparently impressed, for a new order was issued to the judges that death sentences should be given only for very serious offences. For lesser crimes, transportation was to be imposed.

I make the following fact a present to those who so ardently fight for the abolition of capital punishment; that, with the decrease of hanging as a punishment for minor crimes, there was also a decrease in the more violent type of crime.

In the year 1802 occurred one of the most dramatic trials and horrible executions ever known in the Old Bailey. Governor Joseph Wall was tried and sentenced for the murder of Benjamin Armstrong twenty years before. He had committed a cruel and fearsome murder, and it was a cruel and fearsome end—though thoroughly deserved—which he was called upon to face on a cold snowy morning in January, 1802.

There is no gainsaying that Wall was a brave and resourceful soldier, who had rendered great service to his country; but he was also an adventurer. Having met a Miss Gregory of Dublin, whom he wooed with more vigour than tenderness, he was mulcted in damages for assaulting her.

To avoid paying these, the ungallant Lothario fled Dublin for England, where he obtained the Governorship of the island of Goree off the coast of Africa.

Here, his quarrelsome disposition and fierce temper made him disliked by all. At length, worn out by the climate of this "white man's grave", he was due to return to England when there occurred the incident which was to end in his public execution thousands of miles from where his crime was committed.

Some men of the Africa Corps came to him about certain money which had been stopped from their pay. Their spokesman was Benjamin Armstrong, who put his case with every respect and deference.

Later, in a flaming temper, Wall ordered a parade of the men under his command; a gun carriage was brought out and Armstrong was ordered to stand forth. Six black slaves tied him securely to the gun-carriage and Wall gave the order for 800 lashes to be applied.

The six slaves used ropes' ends nearly an inch thick, which bruised rather than cut into the flesh of the writhing Armstrong. At every twenty-five lashes a fresh slave was called upon to take up the lashing, so that there should be no slackening of the punishment through tiredness. If one showed signs of flagging, Wall cried out with ferocious enjoyment, "Lay on, you black beasts. Lay on, or I'll lay on you. Cut him to the heart; cut his liver out."

Five days after Wall left Goree, Armstrong died from the terrible beating he had received. That was in 1782. Two years later Wall was arrested in Bath, but managed to elude his escort at Reading, and fled to France where he remained for some years under an assumed name. Then in 1801, with foolhardy effrontery, he returned to England and wrote to the Secretary of State saying he was prepared to submit himself to trial.

Behold him then at the Old Bailey, where he declared that Armstrong was the ringleader of an open mutiny. He denied that he had ever blown men from a cannon, which was alleged against him; but there was so much evidence of his sadistic brutality that the jury could do no other than find him Guilty, and he was sentenced to death.

Through Dr Ford—perhaps the most notorious of Newgate Ordinaries—J. T. Smith, formerly Keeper of the Print Room at the British Museum, was present at the execution of Governor Wall. Smith described his visit to the death cell in the following words:

"As we crossed the press yard a cock crew, and the solitary clanking of a restless chain was dreadfully horrible . . . The prisoner entered. He was death's counterfeit, tall, shrivelled and pale; and his soul shot so piercingly through the portholes of his head, that the first glance of him nearly terrified me . . . His hands were clasped and he was truly penitent. After the yeoman had told him to stand up, he 'pinioned' him, and tied the cord with so little feeling that the governor, who had not given the wretch the accustomed fee, observed, 'You have tied me very tight,' upon which Dr Ford ordered him to slacken the cord, but not without muttering.

"Then turning to the doctor questioned him, 'Do tell me Sir: I am informed I shall go down with great force; is that so?' "

Dr Ford thereupon explained the working of the new drop, and the victim-to-be then joined the Ordinary in prayer, exhibiting a worthy but belated contrition.

Kirby, the Keeper of Newgate at that time, asked the usual question, "Have you any particular wish?"

"I most earnestly desire that I be not pulled by the legs and that the cord be properly adjusted," replied Wall, causing James Botting the executioner to frown. It seemed to him a reflection on his craftsmanship.

So Joseph Wall began his last short journey on earth. As he made his appearance on the scaffold and gazed at the multitude of faces surrounding him, he glimpsed not one which displayed any sign of sympathy. Not a hat was raised as the noose was adjusted around his neck, and instead of the usual hisses which greeted the hangman, there were cheers for Botting as he worked.

Mumbling his hackneyed prayer, Dr Ford was constantly interrupted by ribald comments from the crowd. Sheriff Cox, in charge of the execution, gave the signal, and Botting stepped forward to release the platform; but either he had fortified himself with too much rum, or was a trifle nervous, for he managed to adjust the knot in such a position that it slipped to the back of Wall's neck. When the trap opened, instead of disappearing through it, Wall was seen spinning round and round in the air, his head ridiculously awry, his body jerking this way and that as he fought for breath.

Nor was his dying wish vouchsafed him, for as one chronicler of the day reports: "The condemned man was seen to struggle much more than has been the case with any other sufferer. At the expiration of eleven minutes it was found necessary to pull his legs; and not till then did he finally cease to breathe."

Less than fifteen minutes later, James Botting was selling for a shilling an inch the rope with which he had hanged Wall. In Newgate Street, an old man of enterprise was selling an identical rope at the cut price of sixpence an inch, while

"Rosy Emma", the reputed wife of Botting, was selling a similar rope at twopence a piece to some buttermen who had come up from Epping to Newgate Market, and tarried to combine the pleasure of seeing Wall hanged with the business of selling their butter.

Five years later, in 1807, it was the throng of drink-maddened onlookers who suffered death and disaster at an execution. Two men named Haggerty and Holloway were found guilty of the murder of Mr Steel, a lavender merchant in the Strand, whose battered body had been found in a gravel pit near Hounslow.

On the day of the execution a crowd of some 80,000 surged into Old Bailey, and even before the prisoners appeared on the scaffold several women were trampled to death. There followed scenes of unparalleled pandemonium; the people were wild with rage and fear; some clambered on to a cart which broke down beneath their weight and launched its human freight into the milling crowd.

In all, twenty-eight people were killed in the scrimmage, and over seventy suffered grave injuries.

Despite general apathy towards reform in this insensitive age, minor improvements in prison life took place. In 1810, for example, debtors were prohibited from having their wives and families to live with them in Newgate; but there was still no restraint on the number of visitors who could enter the prison. Wives and mistresses, some with children at their breasts, came there to spend the day. They filled the corridors and lay about the yards, the babies crying, the women frequently indulging in free fights, and drunken orgies raging the whole day through.

That same year, however, the prison tap-room was closed, and thus there was a little less drinking within prison confines, although liquor could still be obtained if one knew how.

We have already met the Newgate chaplain or Ordinary, Dr Ford, and it may be an appropriate moment to see how that gentleman carried on his religious work among the congregation provided for him in gaol. In a Parliamentary Report of 1814 is the following passage:

"Beyond his attendance at chapel and on those who are sentenced to death Dr Ford feels but few duties to be attached to his office. He knows nothing of the state of morals in the prison; he never sees any of the prisoners in private. Though fourteen boys and girls from nine to thirteen years old were in Newgate in April last, he does not consider attention to them a point of his duty. He does not know that any have been sick until he gets a warning to attend their funeral; and does not go to the infirmary, for it is not in his instructions."

I have mentioned Elizabeth Fry, the great woman reformer who devoted her life to penal reform. She was active about this time in forming the Ladies' Prison Visiting Association.

It was no gentle task that this courageous woman with her worthy helpers undertook; for so terrible were the conditions in the women's part of Newgate that it was known as "hell above ground".

She has left her records of what she saw when she visited Newgate in 1816. She found the inner yard, which abutted on to the street, filled with a struggling mass of half-nude women whose clothes had either fallen off them, or been torn from their skinny bodies in the fight to get near the railings. Here they held out long sticks with spoons attached to the ends, beseeching passers-by to give them money. W. Eden Hooper, in his work on Newgate, describes in graphic detail these hopeless human derelicts.

"Many of them were mad drunk, others sat about the stones, squalid and ferocious. They all dragged heavy leg-irons about with them, riveted to the knees and again to their ankles, being unable to pay for 'easement'. In the wards they slept on the floor, many nearly naked; weak from want of food, savage from drink, unsexed and hopeless."

Those were the women whom Elizabeth Fry sought to

succour, and succour them she did. As Hooper says, "Steadily persisting in the task she had set out to perform, this humane woman quickly brought about an entire change in the habits and persons of her fallen sisters . . . She wooed the women through their innocent offspring . . . In 1817 she formed a school for the children and the younger criminals."

She and her band of fellow-workers almost lived among the prisoners. They secured the appointment of a humane woman who became the first prison matron in the country. They secured wardresses in place of the male officers, who, up to this time, were in charge of the female as well as the male wards.

When Mrs Fry approached members of the City Corporation to have the prison cleaned up, she was told that it was "useless to attempt to reform such untamed and turbulent spirits except by punishment".

But Elizabeth Fry knew what she was about, and it is on record that very soon the female felons' side of Newgate was a different place. The women began to make clothes for their children. They gave up their drink and gambling. The worst of their kind became quiet, orderly and industrious. Many learned to read. A ward woman attended to the cleanliness of the wards. A yard woman saw to it that good order was maintained in the yards. A nurse and assistant kept attendance in the sick room. All of them were prisoners, selected for these responsible tasks because of their respectable habits.

The women grew honest among themselves, and of over 100,000 articles manufactured not one was stolen.

As I said at the beginning of this chapter, I cannot do more than give a passing glimpse of the work of the reformers of that day; and having paid them this all too inadequate tribute, let us pass on once more to the story of the Old Bailey as—even in those days—the greatest criminal court in the world.

CHAPTER TEN

TWO BAD MEN AND SOME OTHERS

PUBLIC executions continued throughout the first half of the 19th century to draw large crowds to the Old Bailey, and Thackeray, who was present in 1840 at the hanging of Courvoisier for the murder of his master Lord William Russell, was impelled to write an essay which appeared in *Fraser's Magazine*. He described the windows surrounding the spot where the gallows was erected as being full of "quiet family parties of honest tradesman, sipping tea with calm, and moustached dandies squirting the throng below with brandy and water".

That was one hundred years ago.

Nine years later Charles Dickens denounced the scenes at the execution of Mr and Mrs Manning for the murder of the woman's lover, Patrick O'Connor.

Dickens had attended the Old Bailey throughout that sensational trial, and had seen the woman fly into a screaming rage as the jury returned their verdict of Guilty. He had seen her fling the little posies of rue, which bedecked the ledge of the dock, at the black-capped judge as he passed sentence of death.

Later, Dickens attended the last act in this drama. He saw Maria Manning mount the scaffold (outside the old Horsemonger Lane Gaol on this occasion) clad in a fine black satin dress which gleamed even in the sombre light of the morning. She showed nothing but contemptuous scorn for those gathered there to watch her die.

But—black satin went out of fashion for nearly thirty years.

Dickens was horrified at what he saw during that long night. In a letter to the *Times* written the next day, he said:

"I believe that a sight so inconceivably awful as the wickedness and levity of the crowd collected at the execution this morning, could be imagined by no man, and could be presented in no heathen land under the sun . . . When I came upon the scene at midnight, the shrilling of the cries and howls which were raised from time to time, denoting that they came from boys and girls assembled in the best places, made my blood run cold . . . When the day dawned, thieves, low prostitutes, ruffians and vagabonds of every kind, flocked to the ground with every variety of offensive and foul behaviour. Fightings, fainting, imitations of Punch, brutal jokes, tumultuous demonstrations of indecent delight, when swooning women were dragged out of the crowd by the police with their dresses disordered, gave a new zest to the general entertainment . . . When the two miserable creatures who attracted all this ghastly sight about them were turned quivering into the air, there was no more emotion, no more pity, no more thought that two immortal souls had gone to judgment, no more restraint of any of the previous obscenities, than if the name of Christ had never been heard in this world, and there were no belief among men but that they perished like beasts . . .

"I am solemnly convinced that nothing that ingenuity could devise to be done in this city, in the same compass of time, could work such ruin as one public execution, and I stand astounded and appalled by the wickedness it exhibits."

Charles Dickens' son, the late Sir Henry Fielding Dickens, sat as Common Serjeant at the Old Bailey for many years administering the more humane justice which his illustrious father had fought so hard to bring about.

Another twenty years were to elapse before the last public execution took place in that thoroughfare known as the Old Bailey. But I shall have more to say about that at the proper time.

In the meantime, in the year 1843, there had occurred one of the most momentous trials in the history of the Old Bailey.

To-day, whenever the defence of insanity is raised at a murder trial, there is invariably a reference to the McNaughton Rules, for it was as a result of the jury's verdict of Not Guilty, on the ground of insanity in that case, that all the judges were called upon to attend at the House of Lords to decide what should in future be considered the legal definition of insanity.

The trial itself had aroused tremendous interest. McNaughton was a Glasgow wood-turner who laboured under a delusion that he had a grievance against Sir Robert Peel, the then Prime Minister. One night, as one Edward Drummond left the office of Sir Robert at 10 Downing Street, McNaughton crept up behind him with a loaded pistol and shot him dead. He declared afterwards that he thought Drummond was Sir Robert Peel whom he intended to kill.

The medical evidence was very strong and definite that the prisoner was insane, and the jury brought in a verdict to the effect.

Public feeling was strong on the point of McNaughton's responsibility or irresponsibility for his act, and it was felt that some definite ruling should be laid down. The question was debated in the House of Lords, and then the judges were summoned, five set questions being put to them on which to express their opinions. There is no need to enter into all the questions, or the details of the discussion. The final decision arrived at by the learned judges was to the following effect:

> That no act is a crime if the person who commits it is, at the time, prevented by any disease of the mind from:
> (1) Knowing the nature and quality of his act.
> (2) Knowing that the act is wrong, or
> (3) Controlling his own conduct, unless the absence of control has been produced by his own default.

The effect of this ruling was of vital importance from a legal aspect. In the first place it put upon the defence the onus of proving the accused to be insane. The Lord Chief Justice of that day (Tindal), who delivered the opinion of the judges, made it abundantly clear when he stated:

"Every man is presumed sane, and to possess a sufficient degree of reason to be responsible for his crimes, until the contrary is proved; *and that to establish a defence on the ground of insanity, it must be clearly proved that, at the time of the commission of the act, the party accused was labouring under such a defect of reason, from disease of the mind, as not to know the nature and quality of the act he was doing; or, if he did know it, that he did not know he was doing what was wrong.*"

I may mention that the McNaughton findings have for years past been a subject of legal controversy, and such eminent jurists as the late Lord Birkenhead, the late Mr Justice Avory and the late Lord Darling have expressed themselves very strongly on the legal definition of insanity. Lord Darling attempted to deal with the matter in a special Bill, which, however, came to an untimely end.

The McNaughton ruling is still the basis of our law as regards insanity.

Let us turn now to the "bad men" of my chapter heading, and consider the case of William Palmer, the infamous Rugely poisoner.

Palmer was a doctor who forsook medicine for the race-course except when he found it profitable to administer strychnine either to remove pressing creditors, or inherit legacies which he had thoughtfully engineered.

There was nothing sinister about the appearance of Palmer. He was of rubicund complexion, with a round, cheery face and pleasant, companionable manner. Born in Rugely, he set up in practice there after taking his diploma. In marrying a daughter of a Colonel Brookes, Palmer made his first error, not because she was an undutiful wife, but because the money he thought she would inherit on the death of her father did not materialise. Colonel Brookes certainly left a substantial fortune, but it turned out that Palmer's wife was illegitimate, and the real heirs secured the bulk of the money.

In view of his expectations Palmer began his young life on a spendthrift scale, nor did he economise when he found things going badly with him. Instead, he plunged more heavily into racing, owned and bred racehorses, and laid big bets. Once the idea of poisoning had taken shape in his mind, he began to regard it as a solution of all difficulties. There is little doubt that in 1849 he poisoned his mother-in-law when she came to them on a visit, so that he might obtain some property in Stafford. In 1850, one of his turf friends, named Bladen, stayed with him in Rugely, but did not leave the house alive. He had just won a huge sum of money which he took with him to Rugely. It was known also that Palmer owed him for several big bets. But neither the money, nor the book containing details of Palmer's indebtedness, was found.

No matter how much money he had, Palmer never found it enough, and by the year 1853 he was in debt to bill-discounters for over £12,000. In the following year he forged his own mother's signature to bills for that amount. He also forged other acceptances in the name of one of his best friends, John Parsons Cook.

Meanwhile he insured the life of his wife with different offices for a total sum of £13,000, and was negotiating further proposals with other companies when his wife died suddenly. The insurance companies paid out, but even so large a sum could not redeem all Palmer's bills. So he took out another series of policies, this time on the life of his brother.

Again, the total sum amounted to £13,000—a most unlucky number for both insured and insurer as things turned out—for when the brother died and the poisoner put in his claim, the companies refused to pay.

It was the week of the Shrewsbury races, and Palmer was desperate. He attended the meeting with his friend Cook, who won some large bets. Palmer was not so fortunate. On November 13, Cook's horse Polestar won the cup and some £700 on the main event. Cook had the money on him when he dined that night with Palmer at the Raven Hotel. Palmer stood him a drink which, Cook said, tasted funny. Cook was taken ill, recovered slightly when Palmer was not about, but had a relapse immediately the doctor began to tend him again. Palmer left Cook in the hands of an aged doctor while he went up to London.

That morning he had received notice that the moneylenders who had discounted bills for £4,000 on the forged signature of Palmer's mother, had issued writs against them both. He was at his wits' end. He got a friend in London to go to Tattersalls with forged authority from Cook to draw his winnings, and then sent the money round to the moneylenders to hold them off for a time.

Then he returned to Rugely, and with every apparent tenderness looked after his sick friend, plying him with broth and milk and medicine. But Cook died in terrible agony, his body contorted and stiffened, his eyes staring, his arms twisted as he passed away in painful spasms.

It was not until the examination of Cook's papers and a search of Palmer's house revealed the latter's financial difficulties, that suspicion was aroused, and foul play suspected. In a medical book left open at a page dealing with strychnine, was a note in Palmer's own hand-writing. It read: "Kills by tetanic action, the muscles."

So Palmer was arrested and brought to trial for Cook's murder. Until that time it was the invariable custom for a person charged with murder to be tried at the Assize for the county in which the crime had been committed, but so great was the feeling against Palmer in Staffordshire that it was clear there was no possibility of an impartial trial in his home county. A special Act of Parliament was passed enabling his trial to be held at the Old Bailey.

It was the first trial for poisoning by strychnine ever held in England, and naturally attracted much attention. Attorney-General Cockburn, afterwards Lord Chief Justice of England, prosecuted, and three judges presided. They were Chief Justice Campbell, Mr Justice Cresswell, and Mr Baron Alderson.

You may gather that the judge was not too kindly inclined towards Palmer, by the contents of a note which the prisoner passed down to his counsel, which read, "I wish there was two-and-a-half grains of strychnine in old Campbell's acidulated draught; solely because I think he acts unfairly."

A packed court of society leaders, princes, lords and fashionable ladies were present as audience to the grim drama. Again, only the one charge was investigated, but almost everyone knew the victims of the dapper little man in the dock numbered something like fourteen or fifteen, including his own wife and brother. In consequence there was little sympathy when at length he was sentenced to death, or when he was "taken back to the place from whence he came" to be "hanged by the neck" before a concourse of some 50,000 people outside Stafford Gaol.

There had been some attempt, about that time, to improve both the buildings of Newgate and the Old Bailey court, and the circumstances under which prisoners were brought to trial. After the Central Criminal Court Act of 1834 had been passed, the Old Bailey was remodelled, and it was ordered that Sessions should be held at least twelve times a year—as they are to-day. A third court was added to expedite trials, so that prisoners would not have to wait such a long time on remand.

All prisoners awaiting trial came before the court at the sessions after their committal, unless the prosecution could show good cause why the trial should be postponed until the next sessions.

The population of Newgate was kept down to some extent by this monthly clearance, although even then there was insufficient accommodation to carry on all the business of the courts. Hence another minor rebuilding operation in 1856 —soon after the Palmer trial—when it was decided that in future Newgate should be used only as a "holding" prison for those awaiting trial, in precisely the same way that Brixton Gaol is to-day used as a holding or remand prison.

There were corresponding improvements in the Old Bailey as well; but unfortunately there was little improvement in the conduct of trials. The bullying methods of Old Bailey counsel and their lack of restraint in dealing with witnesses, earned for many of them a bad name. Comparison with an Old Bailey counsel was a recognised term of reproach. The art of advocacy has reached a higher stage to-day, and there is now little cause for complaint.

Although the first railway for passenger traffic in England was opened in 1825, almost forty years elapsed before the first train murder was committed. That was in July, 1864, when Thomas Briggs was found battered to death in a railway carriage.

I only mention this case in passing, because it made history as the first train murder in England, and because Franz Muller, the murderer, was tried at the Old Bailey.

In 1864 a Commission on Capital Punishment was appointed, and one can imagine the controversy which went on in the Press of that day. Charles Dickens was again well to the fore in this campaign and there is little doubt that his mighty pen was one of the weapons which brought about the abolition of public executions in 1868.

The last person to be executed in public was Michael Barrett, who was hanged for his connection with a Fenian plot to blow up Clerkenwell House of Detention, where two men, Burke and Casey, were confined on a charge of treason-felony.

The plot was formed among the Fenians of London and Manchester to liberate their comrades, and a barrel of gunpowder was placed against a wall of the prison, and exploded. The result was terrible. Many nearby houses were blown to pieces and four people killed outright. Some forty others were maimed or wounded, some of them fatally. Most of the victims were women and children.

Neither Burke nor Casey gained his liberty, and five men and a woman, Barrett among them, were arrested and eventually brought to trial on a charge of murdering Sarah Ann Hodgkinson, one of the victims of the explosion. (The case against the woman was withdrawn after evidence.)

Of the five who were put on trial, Barrett was the only one found Guilty, the others being acquitted. A less murderous face than Barrett's was never seen in the dock at the Old Bailey. It expressed good-humour, frankness and intelligence. After the verdict he was asked whether he had anything to say, and in one of the most amazing extempore speeches ever heard in court, he courteously, and without bravado, addressed the judges. With infinite skill he analysed the evidence against him, denying that his was the hand that fired the barrel.

He wound up with a peroration during which men and women openly wept, the sobs of the women punctuating his speech. Two or three fainted and had to be carried out, so great was the emotional stress caused by his eloquence.

"If it is murder to love Ireland more dearly than life, then indeed I am a murderer," he said. "If I could in any way remove the miseries or redress the grievances of that land by the sacrifice of my own life I would willingly, nay gladly do so. If it should please the God of Justice to turn to some account, for the benefit of my suffering country, the sacrifice of my poor, worthless life I could, by the Grace of God, ascend the scaffold with firmness, strengthened by the consoling reflection that the stain of murder did not rest upon me, and mingling my prayers for salvation of my immortal soul with those for the regeneration of my country."

Even that hard-bitten lawyer, Lord Chief Justice Cockburn, who, with Baron Bramwell, presided at the trial, betrayed great emotion during Barrett's oration.

The Irishman met his death with the same placid calm as he had revealed during his trial.

That was in May, 1868.

The first execution held in private at Newgate Gaol took place in the following September. The murderer was Alexander Mackay, who killed his mistress by beating her with a rolling pin and a furnace rake.

It is interesting to note the contrast in the atmosphere at the hanging of Mackay. Instead of the raucous shouts and fair-ground behaviour of seething crowds, there were only a few officials present, and they went about their tasks in an awed silence. One or two of them became physically sick, and Mackay himself broke down and had to be supported to the gallows. It may have been the silent horror of the scene which brought about his collapse.

In 1877 there occurred an incident which was the indirect cause of the ultimate demolition of Newgate Gaol. This was a fire which broke out in the Sessions House and did so much damage that the City Lands Committee were ordered to make a report on what they considered necessary to provide adequate and suitable accommodation for the proper holding of prisoners awaiting trial, and for despatching the increased business of the courts.

That same year was passed the Prisons Act which came into operation in April, 1878. Under this Act the Male Wing of Newgate Gaol was taken over by the Government. Newgate had already ceased to be used as a prison for debtors and Sir William Harcourt, the then Home Secretary, ordered that it should cease to be used as a regular prison, *except as a place of confinement for prisoners convicted of capital offences at the Old Bailey, and awaiting execution.*

In 1878 the City Lands Committee reported that the only way to carry out these reforms properly was to pull down the old Sessions House and build new courts and offices on its site, and adjoining premises. Many years passed before the authorities made up their minds that Newgate had outgrown its use and was altogether redundant. It was ten years before the Common Council ordered an enquiry into the practicability of building a more modern and enlarged Old Bailey Sessions House on the site of the disused Newgate Prison. And it was another ten years before the Home Secretary agreed with the suggestion.

Arrangements were finally concluded in September, 1901, and designs were invited for the proposed new building. The plans submitted by Mr E. W. Mountford, F.R.I.B.A., were selected.

But again we are leaping ahead of our story. Let us turn to the second of the two bad men who form the subject of my chapter title.

Dr Neill Cream was a cross-eyed, ugly Lothario whose attraction for women is past all understanding. The son of a Scotsman living in Canada, he took his M.D. at Montreal University. Before going to Canada, however, he had "walked" St Bartholomew's Hospital—just across the road from the Old Bailey where he was tried—and had also studied medicine at Edinburgh where he obtained the M.R.C.S. and L.R.C.P. diplomas in the name of Thomas Neill.

Before he came to London he had applied his knowledge of poisons with effect. He poisoned the girl-wife whom he had been compelled to marry by an irate father in Toronto, and, as she lay dying in his arms, had sobbed out his heart in apparent grief.

He then departed to Illinois where he came upon an elderly rancher named Stott whom he poisoned with strychnine. He forced Stott's young wife to give herself to him on pain of being denounced as the murderess of her husband. To compel the wife's compliance, however, he wrote a note to the authorities, declaring that in his opinion Stott had died from strychnine poisoning. The police took a serious view of his knowledge, and Cream was charged with the murder of the man, and spent ten years in an American penitentiary.

Letter-writing seems to have been Cream's weakness. His subsequent arrest in London for the murder of four women, with a further charge of attempting to murder another two, was brought about through letter-writing.

On his release from prison in the United States, Cream came to London and within twelve months had poisoned at least six women, four of whom died. He was living in lodgings in Lambeth Palace Road when he met Matilda Clover, who was a woman of the streets, as were all the victims of that other terror murderer, "Jack the Ripper".

Matilda died in terrible agony after Cream had visited her at her lodgings, but there was no suspicion about her death at the time, as another doctor's assistant had given a certificate stating that the girl had died from *delirium tremens.*

A day or two before this incident, Ellen Dodworth had been found writhing in agony, and convulsively struggling with some people, in Waterloo Road. She died in hospital, but not before she had mentioned that "a tall, dark man gave me a drink out of a bottle. He had a squint."

We now get another glimpse of Cream's mania for letter-writing. It may have been the vanity of the criminal, for most criminals think they are inordinately brilliant, but whatever the reason, the fact is Cream wrote to the Coroner offering to produce information which would lead to the arrest of the murderer of Dodworth, if the Government would pay him £300,000. The letter containing this modest claim was signed "A. O'Brien, detective".

There followed a spate of letters to various people, including such public figures as Mr F. W. D. Smith, a partner in the famous firm of booksellers, charging him with the murder of poor Ellen, and offering immunity at a specified figure. Lady Russell, wife of Sir Charles Russell, was informed that her husband had murdered Clover, and other prominent people received similar disturbing epistles; all in a disguised hand, but all containing the Greek Σ, which was a characteristic of Cream's handwriting.

How largely these letters contributed to Cream's undoing may be judged from the fact that until they were received, *there had been no suspicion that Clover had died from strychnine poisoning.*

Why did he write them? I can only conjecture that his mind was crazed through the drugs he took to still his conscience. His landlady told of the fearful shrieks which came from his room in the dead of night; when, perhaps, he was living in himself the physical agony which he must have known his victims had suffered, or were perhaps even then suffering.

Meanwhile he took a short trip to the United States, returning with some 500 strychnine pills. Two days after his return, two women named Shrivel and Marsh, who lived in Stamford Street, were found dying from strychnine poisoning. A man answering the description of Dr Neill had been seen just before dawn, leaving the house where the two women lived.

Justice was creeping towards the poisoner. Living in the same house with him at Lambeth Palace Road was a young medical student named Harper. Cream accused him of murdering the four women who had died of strychnine poisoning. He also wrote to Harper's father offering to keep silent in return for £1,500. But Mr Harper was wise enough to go to the police and place the letter in the hands of Inspector Trowbridge, who had the enquiries in hand.

Then Cream did another stupid thing. He told his landlady's daughter of his "suspicions", and in consequence, when the police began to make enquiries, they were inevitably led to Dr Neill and the latter was arrested.

Cream persisted in his folly, and not only declared that Harper had slain the four dead women, but also mentioned that the youth had murdered one Lou Harvey. This was a bad slip, for *Lou Harvey was not dead.* The strychnine pills which Cream had given her while they were walking together on the Embankment—and which, by the time of his arrest, should have done their agonising work—had not been swallowed, but thrown away. So there was Lou, ready to come forward and identify the accused.

The trial of Cream before Mr Justice Hawkins was a battle of the experts, but it was the evidence of Lou Harvey which finally placed the rope around the murderer's neck; that and the accusing letters written to others, with the unmistakable Greek Σ.

When the judge put on the black cap to pass sentence of death, police crowded round the dock. It was a precautionary move, for Cream had declared that in such an event he would kill the judge by "some unseen agency". But the agency was evidently not working on this occasion, for nothing happened, and in due course Cream mounted the scaffold and was hanged.

Passing over the oft-told story of Millsom and Fowler and their dramatic fight in the dock, together with the trial of Mrs Dyer, the Reading baby farmer, I would like to close this chapter with the mention of one who made history, but whose name never achieved the headlines.

George Woolfe murdered Charlotte Cheesewright in the year 1902, and in May of that year achieved the unhappy distinction of being the *last* person to be hanged in Newgate Gaol.

Of the details of his crime I can tell you nothing. It was a murder of little legal importance. But still, Woolfe made history, for in that same year the contractors began their demolition of this plague spot in the history of crime and punishment. Until the new Old Bailey was built, trials took place in the stuffy, dingy, and insanitary old court-rooms of the Old Sessions House just down the road from the doomed Newgate Gaol.

Here it seems appropriate to mention "Dead Man's Walk", that dank, sinister-looking, last walking place of those awaiting execution, and their ultimate burial place.

This walk—sometimes known as "Birdcage Walk" because

of its latticed iron roof—was a long, stone-walled corridor, with heavy flag-stones for its floor. It was covered with the grime and dirt of centuries when I saw it just before the demolition gang began their work. Even so, it was possible to discern some of the initials carved on its walls, marking the burial place of those who had died on the scaffold.

Some of these initials were centuries old, and their owners had long since passed from memory when I saw them.

At the end of the corridor stood the condemned cell from which a prisoner made his last journey to the scaffold, and it is along this half-dark corridor that many a prisoner has, knowingly or unknowingly, on his last earthly journey walked over the very spot destined to be his grave.

CHAPTER ELEVEN

FAREWELL TO THE "OLD" OLD BAILEY

I COME now to the period when I first made acquaintance with the Old Bailey; a period of which I can write from experience. And, lest any sinister impression be gathered from this statement, I hasten to add that I was never in the dock on a criminal charge.

It is some forty-eight years since I attended my first trial at the *old* Sessions House, and wended my way up the ill-lit stairs into the musty court. It was a trial of little importance as trials go, a simple case of larceny, quickly disposed of.

Two years later I was present at a trial which aroused world-wide interest, and in spite of the fact that the case of Adolf Beck has been described over and over again, the story of the Old Bailey would not be complete without some brief reference to it. This case will always be regarded as the classic example of mistaken identity resulting in one of the gravest miscarriages of justice ever known.

Beck was twice arrested on charges of stealing money and jewellery from a number of women. The first time, in 1896, he was sent to penal servitude for seven years. The second time, in 1904, he had been found guilty of similar offences, and was actually awaiting sentence, when the extraordinary incident happened which proved him to have been twice wrongly convicted for another man's crime.

The evidence on which Beck had been found Guilty was, in both instances, his identification by a number of women. They stated that they knew him as a man who, posing as the "Earl of Wilton" or "Lord Winton de Willoughby", had borrowed money, or had taken their trinkets on the pretext of buying them more suitable jewellery. In addition there were letters and cheques, the hand-writing on which was identified by eminent experts, including Mr. Gurrin, as that of Adolf Beck.

The incident to which I have referred was a chance visit to Tottenham Court Road Police Station by Inspector Kane of Scotland Yard. He learned that a man named Thomas had been arrested in the act of pawning two rings belonging to two sisters. The story Thomas had told the women was strangely familiar, and the detective went to have a look at the man in his cell. He noticed a scar on Thomas's jaw which had been mentioned more than once at the Beck trials, and any remaining doubts were swept away when Kane saw letters written to the women by Thomas. *The handwriting was identical in every respect with that which had helped to convict Beck at both his trials.*

Kane immediately reported his discovery to the authorities, and the innocence of Beck was quickly established. He was at once released and Free Pardons granted him. An offer of £2,000 compensation was made, which Beck refused. A Committee of Enquiry was demanded by the public, whose sense of justice had been outraged by the knowledge of poor Beck's sufferings, and Beck was eventually awarded the sum of £5,000 to assuage his indignation and compensate him for his long, wrongful imprisonment.

Thomas was proved to be the man who had carried out similar frauds and thefts in 1877, and also on the occasion of Beck's arrest and imprisonment in 1896. But for Kane's lucky visit to the police station, Beck might have suffered yet another long term of penal servitude.

Fortunately, cases of mistaken identity carrying such tragic results are rare, although another instance that comes to mind is that of George Edalji, who, only a year or two before Beck's deliverance, had been sent to penal servitude for seven years as a result of what was called the "Great Wyrley Cattle Maiming" case.

George Edalji was a young Parsee solicitor at the time of these outrages, in which, night after night—with due warning to the local police—horse after horse was found disembowelled and dead or dying in different fields.

Arrested, brought to trial and convicted, Mr Edalji served four years of his sentence, before the agitation led by the late Sir Arthur Conan Doyle secured his release from gaol, together with a Free Pardon. His name was also restored to the roll of solicitors, a sufficient proof that his innocence had been thoroughly established. In this case no compensation was granted. Mr Edalji is still alive and still practising at this time, and I have chatted with him quite recently.

It was Sir Arthur Conan Doyle, too, who was largely instrumental in getting quashed the conviction of Oscar Slater for the murder of Miss Marion Gilchrist, after Slater had served eighteen years' imprisonment. Again, two women had made a mistake in their identification of Slater. One woman, Helen Lambie—long years afterwards—confessed that she had *not* recognised Slater as the murderer, in spite of swearing she had at his trial, but *had* recognised someone else. Slater was released, and given £6,000 compensation. He died a few years ago.

I am not likely to forget the first big murder trial I attended at the Old Bailey. It was on a stifling hot day in July, 1905, when Arthur Devereux, a chemist, stood charged with the murder by poisoning of his wife and children. I can see him now with his blue eyes blandly gazing out at judge and jury, or narrowing as he fenced with Mr Charles Matthews, counsel for the prosecution.

I have never been able to fathom the motive for his crime, unless it was a combination of jealous love for Stanley, his six-years-old son, and his obvious dislike of the twin babies born in 1902.

The facts are these: after a term of imprisonment for fraud and false pretences, Devereux made detailed preparations to kill his wife and babies. First he took a second floor flat, paying the landlord extra rent so that the flat beneath should not be let. He then proceeded to poison his wife and younger children with chloroform and morphia, sparing the eldest boy, Stanley. Next he placed the bodies of all three in a tin trunk which he locked and deposited in a warehouse, declaring that it was filled with books and chemicals, and that he wanted to store it until he was settled in his new house.

I can still hear the thin, reedy voice of "Charlie" Matthews, as he cross-examined Devereux on the gruesome details of the disposal of the bodies. Yet the accused never once blanched at the grisly memories which must have been evoked in his mind.

"Was it your wife you put first in the trunk?" asked Counsel. "Yes," was the reply.

"Who carried the body from the front door to the back?" ——"I did."

Detail after detail was elicited of that terrible scene in the chamber of death, and still Devereux did not flinch.

Counsel produced a copy of the *Chemist and Druggist*, advertising for an assistant to start work at Hull some time in March.

"Did you reply to that advertisement on January 22 saying you were a widower with one child?"

"Yes, by telegram," was the answer—as damning a reply as was ever made by a man on trial for his life.

January 22 *was at least a week before the murder had been committed. What was more, counsel had a copy of the telegram which read;* "Will a widower with one child aged six suit?"

You may wonder what was Devereux's explanation of these extraordinary happenings.

He said that he returned from a walk with his son Stanley one evening, to find that his wife had killed herself and her two babies. He became panic stricken, and made preparations to dispose of the bodies lest he should be accused of the crime.

Mr George Elliott, defending counsel, made an impassioned appeal in his closing speech for his client.

"This is no ordinary man," he said. "His self-confessed

conduct has shown him to be, in one respect, a monster in human form. Horrible and repulsive beyond conception is his admission that after his awful discovery he slept in the bed in which his dead wife had lain a few moments before.

"There is still sanctuary for him—the sanctuary of your merciful consideration, whose door whispering justice will not allow you to close while there remains one lingering doubt of guilt."

But nothing could have saved Devereux, and the jury were only absent five minutes on this occasion, before bringing in the verdict which rid the world of one of its worst murderers.

That was one of the first of 317 murder trials which I have attended in the last forty years. It remains fresh in my mind to this day.

Let us leap over the next two years and come to that dismal day in March, 1907, when the last trials were heard in the old Sessions House. It was a momentous day in many respects, for on the previous day King Edward VII had opened the new Central Criminal Court, and had singled out Mr Charles Matthews for the honour of a knighthood, to be bestowed there and then.

The only sword available was the Sword of Justice which hung on the wall over the Judge's seat in the old Court House. This was used, and when Sir Charles Matthews entered the court the next day to prosecute a young man in what was known as the "Brixton Love Tragedy", it was the first case in which he appeared with his title.

We need not go into all the details of that crime in which a young man had murdered his sweetheart, but I would like to give the tribute which Mr George Elliott, who appeared for the defence, paid to Sir Charles for the manner in which he had conducted the prosecution. After having congratulated him on "the signal honour conferred upon him by the King", he continued, "His command of language and his wonderful power of delineation found full expression in placing before you simply and fairly, yet justly and firmly, the case against my client."

The prisoner was found Guilty and sentenced to death, but was afterwards reprieved.

There was one other charge on the judge's list—that of a woman charged with arson, a serious offence carrying a heavy punishment. Perhaps it was fitting that Mr Justice Ridley, who tried that case, should acquit the woman on the grounds that the evidence against her was not reliable. It was a portent that justice would be administered with mercy in the new court.

After he had told the prisoner that she was free, the judge rose and bowed to the court; then as he turned towards the door leading from the Bench, he smiled and remarked, "Gentlemen, I am discharged."

A little later the sword which had hung upon those walls for so many years was lifted down, and placed over the judge's seat in Number One Court of the new building. And what a difference there was between old and new. In place of the narrow, stifling dinginess of the old building were stately halls with fine frescoes. Statues stood in various niches, and a wide marble staircase led up from the lower hall to the domed and well-lit hall from which entrance to the four main courts is gained.

The Courts themselves are of plain oak, yet, in spite of their unpretentious appearance, there is a dignity, almost a majesty, about them, which impresses one from the moment of entry.

CHAPTER TWELVE

OLD BAILEY TRADITION

THE Corporation of the City of London is responsible for the maintenance and upkeep of the Old Bailey. Not a penny is charged to the ratepayer or taxpayer. The whole cost—of the building, as well as its maintenance—comes out of the private funds of the City Corporation. It is a burden at once gladly and proudly borne. In fact, the Corporation has actually declined to be relieved of the burden, so jealous is the City of its ancient honour.

In the early part of the 10th century, the City authorities carried out judicial functions in criminal matters under a body of civic law known as the *Judicia Civitatis Lundonie*. When William the Conqueror became King, he agreed that the City should retain all its legal privileges and customs in return for the surrender of England's capital.

In 1132, Henry I gave a charter to the people of London, authorising them to elect their own Justiciar "for keeping Pleas of the Crown", this document emphasising "that none other should be justice over them".

In a later charter—that of 1461—it was decreed that the Lord Mayor should always be named Justice of Gaol Delivery for Newgate, and he is so named to this day. That is the responsibility carried by each occupant of this ancient office, a responsibility confirmed centuries later by the Central Criminal Court Act, passed by Parliament in 1834.

To say that he "lords" it over the City of London is a truism. The Old Bailey is policed by the City Constabulary, not the Metropolitan Police. The Lord Mayor is invested with the right to "try, hear and determine" all offences which come within jurisdiction of the Old Bailey, and his authority within

City bounds is almost as great as that of the King.

He is also Admiral of the Port of London, with jurisdiction over the tidal waterway between Havengore Creek, in Essex, and Teddington. He may, by right, seek private audience of the King at any time as an *ex-officio* member of the Privy Council, and his rank is that of an Earl.

In days gone by, before Newgate Gaol was demolished, he had a duplicate set of keys to all prison gates and cells, and to-day enjoys right of entry to the Tower of London at any hour of the night or day.

If I seem to stress the powers and rights of the Lord Mayor of London, it is because I want to emphasise the antiquity of his office and his duties.

Just before 1834, it was disputed whether the Lord Mayor sat as First Commissioner at the Old Bailey in virtue of the Charter of 1461 or simply on account of the annual commissions which proclaim this office. The Act of 1834 confirmed his ancient privilege, which has remained unchanged.

To emphasise his official position under the Charter for three years after the Act was passed, and until the accession of Queen Victoria in 1837, all prisoners, even though they had been tried by one of His Majesty's Judges, were sentenced by the Recorder of London as the representative of the Lord Mayor.

Of course the Recorder followed the Judges' notes; but it was he, and not the Judges, who reported all convictions for murder to the King in Council, and he who was instructed that the sentences should or should not be carried out. This practice was abolished by the Act of 1837.

The Lord Mayor and his Aldermen usually took only a passive part in the court proceedings, but there were occasions when they exercised their rights as Commissioners of the Court, as for example in the case of Elizabeth Canning, who was tried and found guilty of perjury in 1745.

Chief Justice Willes was about to award a sentence of

transportation, but a sympathetic Alderman suggested that six months' imprisonment would meet the gravity of the case. The issue was put to the vote but Elizabeth Canning lost the day and was sent overseas to meditate on the evil of lying in court.

The Act of 1834 did more than establish the position of the Lord Mayor; it extended the jurisdiction of the Court. In addition to being the Criminal Court for London and Middlesex, it was empowered to try criminal cases for parts of Essex, Kent and Surrey, and also to try indictments for murder, piracy and felonies committed on the high seas. Thus it became the *Central* Criminal Court, instead of the Criminal Court as it had previously been known.

This far-reaching Act also set down that the Judges of the Old Bailey should be the Lord Mayor (observe how this City dignitary is first named in the enactment), the Lord Chancellor, the Lord Keeper of the Great Seal, the Lord Chief Justice and the existing Judges of the Court of King's Bench, the Dean of Arches, the Aldermen of the City of London, the Judges of the Sheriff's Court (now the Mayor's and City of London Court held at the Guildhall) and any person who has been Lord Chancellor or a Judge of the High Court.

The Dean of Arches is still a judge, and the late Sir Herbert Austin, one of the Court's most illustrious Clerks, humorously suggested one day when business was brisk and judges scarce, "Better send down to St Paul's and ask the Dean of Arches to step along."

The Act laid it down that the presence of two Commissioners was sufficient to constitute a Court. At one time there were three judges sitting at a trial, and doubtless this helped to avoid sentences passed in bias or prejudice. The last time that three judges sat together at the Old Bailey was in 1883, at the trial of the Dynamitards when Lord Coleridge sat with the Master of the Rolls, Sir Baliol Brett, and Mr Justice Grove.

To-day it is the rule that in addition to the Judge sitting

Central Criminal Court in the early 20th century. The inscription over the main entrance reads: "Defend the children of the poor and punish the wrongdoer"

Photo: Bedford Lemere

on the Bench, there must also be another Commissioner within the precincts of the Court.

Only once has this rule occasioned any trouble. This was in 1868, when the notorious Madame Rachel, beauty specialist, blackmailer, swindler and procuress, was sentenced to five years' penal servitude for defrauding one of her clients.

Commissioner Kerr, the judge who tried the case, was on the Bench throughout the trial, but the second Commissioner was not there continuously, but left the precincts of the Court on several occasions, thus leaving only one judge to preside.

Rachel's legal advisers were quick to seize upon this technical breach, and moved for a writ of error in the Queen's Bench. The appeal was duly heard, but it went against the lady, who departed to old Millbank Prison to serve her five years' sentence.

Mention must be made here of yet another personage who plays an equally important if less picturesque part in the administration of justice at the Old Bailey.

The Clerk of the Court is the Chief Executive Officer of the Courts. He holds an onerous position, for he is not only responsible for the smooth running of all the Courts at each session of the Old Bailey, but also for the correctness of the indictments drawn up against every prisoner who comes there.

Judges often consult him on precedents and points of law, and those of you who may have been present at a trial in Number One Court may have seen the presiding judge lean forward over his desk, while the Clerk sitting immediately below stands up on his chair and holds a whispered conversation with his lordship.

Usually the conversation is not about some abstruse point of law, but a question of "What can we do in this case?", not so much a matter of "How much can we give?"—the learned judge knows all the penalties which can be awarded for the various misdemeanours and felonies which come before him—but, "How can we rebuild this man's background?"

For at the Old Bailey the main object is reformation of character, not the blind application of the law.

The present learned Clerk of the Court is Sir Wilfrid Duke Coleridge, son of a famous Lord Chief Justice of that name, who has been associated with the Old Bailey since 1923.

At the opening of each Sessions, the Lord Mayor, followed by his two Sheriffs, sword-bearer and mace-bearer, enters the Court first, even preceding His Majesty's presiding judge. Although the Recorder comes last of all, the office of Recorder of the City of London is almost as ancient as that of the Lord Mayor. He is the principal judicial officer in the City.

The first Recorder of London was one Jeffrey de Norton, Alderman, in 1298, but he had no real legal qualifications, and it was not till a century later, in 1390, that John Tremayne was appointed to the office. He was well-qualified for the position as he had previously been Common Serjeant, a judicial office of even greater antiquity. The precedent of promoting the Common Serjeant to Recorder has been followed many times since that date.

There has been an improvement in remuneration since early days. Originally the salary of the Recorder was £10 per annum. It is now £4,000 a year. The present Recorder is Sir Gerald Dodson, who was one of the finest barristers at the Bar, and is recognised as a judge second to none in his knowledge and application of the law.

In judicial practice there are generally four Judges. There is first of all a Judge of the King's Bench Division, who presides over Number One Court. He is not a permanent judge, but is drawn from the King's Bench each Sessions, so that there is a change every month. Then there are the three permanent judges, including the Recorder, who has his own separate Court, known as Number Two Court. (This was damaged in the Second World War and at the time of writing the Recorder is sitting in Number Four Court.) Next comes the Common

Serjeant, at present Mr Hugh Beazley in Court Number Three, with the additional Judge of the Lord Mayor's, or City of London, Court, now Judge McClure, who sits in Court Number Four.

As I have already mentioned, the Lord Mayor and the Aldermen do not exercise any judicial function, but one of them must be within the precincts of the Court when only one judicial Commissioner is sitting, and they make a brave and picturesque show in their official robes.

The Sword of Justice which hangs in Number One Court, or in the court at which the senior judge is presiding, has been described variously as a golden or jewelled sword of great intrinsic value. I am sorry to have to shatter this illusion. Apart from its priceless worth in tradition, the sword is of no great value. Nor is a great deal known about it beyond a few facts which Mr A. W. Burt, the indefatigable Keeper of the Old Bailey, has managed to dig out from the archives.

According to these, the sword is probably of 16th century date, and may possibly be the "very fayer and goodly sword well and workmanly wrought and gylded", which was given to the City in 1563 by Richard Matthew, citizen and cutler. The haft of the sword has been repaired since that time, and the initials "W.S." now engraved upon it may refer to William Summer, who worked on the sword at nearby Clerkenwell Close, in the year 1806.

This is the sword to which Horatio Bottomley, arch-hypocrite and swindler, pointed as he harangued the jury at the end of his trial for the Victory Bond frauds.

If he were found Guilty, he orated emotionally, that Sword of Justice would fall from its place on the wall.

He *was* found Guilty and sentened to penal servitude for seven years, but the Sword of Justice stayed in its place in Number One Court.

That was in the *new* Old Bailey, and so far we are not yet "off with the old love", so to speak.

At the time of the 1834 Act, which enlarged the jurisdiction of the Court so much, London was still a city of turnpike gates. There was no Charing Cross Railway Station on this side of the river. The railway terminus was then at the Bricklayer's Arms in the Old Kent Road. London's "river taxis", which re-appeared on the Thames in 1948, were thought to be a modern novelty, but about the time of which I write, there were three steamboats, the *Ant*, the *Bee*, and the *Cricket*, on the River Thames. They plied between Hungerford Bridge and London Bridge at one-halfpenny a trip. Strange craft these, for they did not turn round at the end of each journey, but simply returned in reverse, the rudder being shifted from one end to the other.

One of the engineers of the *Cricket* was brought to trial at the Old Bailey after the boiler of the boat had exploded, killing several passengers. An Old Bailey jury found him guilty of manslaughter, and he was duly sentenced.

Late sittings were the rule rather than the exception in those bad old days, and no Judge was more addicted to this practice than Sir Henry Hawkins. At the Penge murder trial, where two brothers named Staunton and two sisters stood charged with the murder of Louis Staunton's wife, Sir Henry began his summing-up at 10 a.m. and continued throughout the day—with only one or two short adjournments—until 10 o'clock the same night. The jury then retired. It was past eleven o'clock when they came back with their verdict of Guilty and sentence of death was passed. (All four were afterwards respited, and sent to penal servitude for life.)

When Lord George Gordon was brought to trial on charges arising from the riots that bore his name, that great Scottish lawyer, Thomas Erskine, who was Lord Chancellor for a time, made an impassioned speech for the prisoner well after midnight. It was not until five in the morning that the jury returned with their verdict of Guilty but Insane.

There is a more leisurely atmosphere about the Old Bailey

in these days. Judges usually rise about 4 p.m. unless by sitting a little later they can finish a case. Every care is taken to ensure that a jury shall not become tired, and unable to give proper attention to the evidence marshalled before it. There is no danger, in these circumstances, of a jury giving a hasty verdict just to get away from the Court.

CHAPTER THIRTEEN

THE "NEW" OLD BAILEY

LORD ALVERSTONE was the Lord Chief Justice at the opening of the *new* Old Bailey in 1907 and naturally it was he who presided at the first Sessions to be held there. He also presided over the first big murder trial to take place in the new building. This was the affair in which William Whiteley, known far and wide as the "Universal Provider", was killed by Horace Rayner, who claimed to be Whiteley's illegitimate son.

Whiteley was not a popular man, except perhaps among the ladies.

Rayner's claim to be the son of Whiteley was false. True, Whiteley *did* have an illegitimate son, and it seemed to Rayner that he had an opportunity to blackmail the wealthy "Universal Provider". He had met Whiteley's illegitimate son, learned something about the circumstances of his birth, and conceived the idea of passing himself off as the young Whiteley.

When he called upon William Whiteley, falsely saying that he had been sent by Sir George Lewis, the famous solicitor, he told a hard-luck story, and asked for financial assistance. Whiteley refused, however, and sent an assistant to call a policeman, whereupon Rayner drew a revolver and shot Whiteley dead, afterwards firing a shot at his own temple, but failing to kill himself.

Rayner's story was that he believed himself to be the son of Whiteley, and that when the dead man refused to help him, and said he had sent for a policeman, his mind became a blank, and he could remember nothing of the tragedy.

He was sentenced to death, but was afterwards reprieved and sent to Broadmoor Criminal Lunatic Asylum, from which he was released in 1919. He died not long afterwards.

Thus the last murderer tried at the old court, and the first murderer sentenced to death at the new court, both escaped the scaffold.

The year 1907 seems full of tense drama as my memory recalls the sensational trials which took place during those twelve months. For instance, there stood in the dock one day a red-haired woman of great beauty. Her smiling face, and expression of childish innocence, gave no inkling of the black record of crime which lay behind her. She was charged under the name of May Vivienne Churchill, but she was known to the police of this country under a dozen aliases, including that of Chicago May.

Beside her in the dock was a weak-mouthed, sullen-looking young man named Charles Smith. They both stood charged with shooting, with intent to kill, the notorious Eddie Guerin, the man who escaped from Devil's Island. I knew Guerin well in after years, when he had fallen on bad times and resorted to petty thieving. He often came to see me to "borrow a dollar or two".

He was a silvery-haired, likeable rascal, and one could not help but feel sorry for him.

Vivienne Churchill's association with Guerin began in the 1890's, when she emigrated from Ireland to New York and became a chorus girl in *The Belle of New York*. She married the son of a well-known business man, but the marriage was a failure, and she became connected with the under-world, and also a dope addict. She drifted from New York to Chicago and there, among the budding Al Capones of that day, became known as Chicago May, because of her desperate exploits.

It was there that Eddie Guerin first met her. He, too, was Irish, and had already served several terms of imprisonment, including one of two years in France. He and the charming May threw in their lot together, returning to London where they embarked on a series of crimes.

With a companion known as Dutch Gus they planned the robbery of the offices of the American Express Company in Paris. The two men forced an entry by night while May kept a vigilant look-out from the street. The robbery was successful but the police got on their track, and all three were arrested.

Guerin was sent to Devil's Island for life. Dutch Gus disappeared. May got five years, afterwards reduced to three. On coming out of gaol she made for London, and there set out on the most ambitious and successful blackmailing campaign ever carried out in the Metropolis. With her male confederates, known as the Northumberland Avenue Gang, she enticed rich and prominent men into compromising situations, and then demanded money on pain of exposure. Scores of letters were found in her possession when she was arrested. Many were written to her by an English peer; there were also letters from other titled men, and yet another of her victims was a famous barrister.

Her blackmail scheme was still operating when Eddie Guerin made his sensational escape from Devil's Isle in 1905. May was living at the time with the weedy but pliable young man, Smith. Two years later, at midnight on June 15, 1907, Guerin and a woman companion were strolling near Russell Square Tube Station when a cab drove up, a woman got out and rushed towards the shelter of a doorway.

"There he is," she cried to her male companion, who had also alighted from the cab. The next moment six revolver shots were fired in rapid succession. The gunman must have been a poor shot, for only one bullet struck Guerin, wounding him slightly in the foot.

A policeman and a civilian gave chase, and Smith—for he was the man who fired the shots—turned the revolver upon them, but without effect; the last shot had been fired. Chicago May was the woman who had cried, "There he is", and both she and Smith were arrested within a few minutes.

They appeared together in the dock at the Old Bailey,

where May was defended by Mr E. D. Purcell, that great advocate for the accused, and Smith by that equally astute counsel Mr Huntley Jenkins. Mr Jenkins set out to prove that Smith had fired the shots, not to kill but to scare Guerin who, it was suggested, intended to throw vitriol over his faithless paramour. Of course, there was not a vestige of truth in the suggestion, nor were the jury hoodwinked into thinking so. Both Chicago May and Smith were found Guilty.

Mr Justice Darling sentenced the woman first—to fifteen years' imprisonment. Chicago May simply smiled as she turned and quietly walked to the cells below.

It was then Smith's turn, and for a moment he stood stunned and unbelieving when the judge awarded him penal servitude for life.

Then an insane frenzy seized him. From his lips came a string of curses and blasphemy, hurled at the judge with all the venom of which he was capable. Gaolers seized him and bundled him rapidly down the steps, but for some seconds, until he was ushered right away from the dock, one could hear his shrill voice raised in vile abuse.

Both were afterwards deported to the States: May, after serving just over ten years of her sentence, and Smith in 1922, after fifteen years' imprisonment.

May died in 1929. Guerin lived on until a few years ago, a tottery, white-haired old man, in and out of prison either as a suspected person, or for picking pockets.

CHAPTER FOURTEEN

SOME COLOURFUL IMPOSTERS

NOT all the trials which took place at the Old Bailey were murder trials, of course, and as my memory roves back over the years I call to mind a procession of rogues and adventurers, male and female, from confidence tricksters to blackmailers; jewel thieves to spies; cat-burglars to passport racketeers; swindlers to pickpockets; fire-bugs to cracksmen.

Some of them were "regulars", old lags who came back time after time. No amount of penal servitude seemed to have any reforming effect. Let us seek a little light relief from the grimmer aspect of the Old Bailey and consider the adventures of those gay deceivers who love nothing better than to assume a grandiloquent title with which to inspire confidence, and so live at the expense of somebody else.

Ernest Dunbar Cairns (or Ernest Edwards or Henry Simpson, it matters not by which name you take him) was one of these. Master-swindler, bankrupt, society pest, pseudo-millionaire and bogus baron, this diminutive man with the black, pointed beard and dark, piercing eyes was as ingenious in the stories he invented to wring money from the unsuspecting as he was in trying to bluff his way out of an awkward corner.

When I saw him at the Old Bailey it was on the simple charge of obtaining credit from London hotels, where he had lived well, without disclosing the fact that he was an undischarged bankrupt. I remembered him of old as the notorious Sugar King who in 1920 had obtained thousands of pounds by the formation of a company called The Mutual Importers Association. He was in Inverness at the time, and publicised a story that he was in a position to supply sugar to the public at 2d. a pound cheaper than the Government-controlled price.

Before this swindle was exposed, Cairns had flown to Devon, where he lived in great style at historic Watermouth Castle, entertaining lavishly and playing lord of the manor for a couple of years. He spent about £20,000 on furniture alone, had a musicians' gallery installed, and even engaged his own private organist. One of the local banks advanced £5,000 to him on overdraft, which of course was not recovered.

When he found that enquiries were being made for him, he chartered a yacht, sailed to Holland where he posed as an American millionaire, and then went on to Brussels in the same guise, adding that he was on a mission from the U.S.A. Government to float loans for the benefit of belligerent countries after the First World War.

In Belgium he was arrested, and sent to prison. Holland afterwards claimed him, and sent him to a lunatic asylum. When he returned to this country—where he had already served terms of imprisonment on various charges of false pretences—he was kept in a mental home for a time. On his release he tried to return to Watermouth Castle, but the steward would not allow him entry. Cairns once again resorted to a few more hotel swindles to make ends meet.

Mad or not, he succeeded in getting a London hotel manager to provide him with a suite of rooms, on the story that he was chairman of the U.S. Refunding Commission, but when his bill reached £43 he could not meet it. Hence his appearance at the Old Bailey, where he insisted that he was the victim of a big political conspiracy.

One of the strangest facts of this case is that Scotland Yard still does not know who he is, nor where he was born, nor how he spent the forty years of his life before he embarked on the series of masquerades which I have mentioned.

Why do men choose this style of life? I have often asked myself this question as I have heard in Court the stories of the crimes and the prison records of these masquerading crooks.

Take Noel Fewsdale Craven, for example. Educated at Bedford Grammar School and London University, a Bachelor of Science, this plausible rogue had every reason to follow a proper career. He was born of respectable parents, was apprenticed to his engineer father, and had a life of useful promise lying before him. Yet he was not far in his 'teens when he first came to the notice of the police and was bound over, there being evidence that he had had some slight mental trouble as a boy.

He then made a journey to Australia and South Africa, but in 1914, after more than one sentence for false pretences, he returned to England. After a further appearance at the Old Bailey he was given another chance, under medical care. He joined the Army, deserted, was court-martialled and discharged. A year later he was charged with unlawfully wearing a naval uniform.

I saw Craven frequently either at the Old Bailey, the London Sessions, or at some other court in the south. Invariably he was charged with hotel bilking, posing as Sir George Carter, Sir Noel Hart, or Sir Norman Stephens, K.B.E. As Sir Norman Stephens, K.B.E., he put up at an exclusive Bournemouth hotel and sent to London for a car with a chauffeur. When the car, valued at £1,135, arrived, "Stephens" gave the chauffeur a bundle of pound notes, and told him to go out and get some new breeches and a shave. When the man returned "Sir Norman" had disappeared with the car. It transpired that he had gone to London, where he stayed with a woman from whom he obtained £60 to tide him over the week-end. He went off the next day and at length reached Clacton. Meanwhile the police were on his track, and they found him surrounded by a group of admiring acquaintances on the steps of an hotel.

"I want you," said one of the officers, and with a smile and wave of the hand to his companions, Craven walked off to another term of imprisonment.

I wonder what has become of Robert Rivett-Carnac, that prince of liars, whom ex-Superintendent Yandell of Scotland Yard once described as a "colossal impostor who invariably poses as a Secret Service agent in the employ of the British Government, when in fact he is antagonistic to the Government. He is a criminal humbug, a pest to society in general, and a danger to the opposite sex in particular."

That statement was made at the Old Bailey, when this sallow-faced and far from prepossessing crook was sent to three years' penal servitude for making a false declaration to secure a marriage licence. But for the timely appearance of Detective-Inspector Yandell (as he was then) on the scene at Doctor's Commons where Carnac stood with his bride-to-be, the latter, a woman doctor of some eminence, might have been yet another victim of this weaver of romantic spells. He had already persuaded her that he was the sole heir of a titled woman who had left him a huge fortune.

It is only proper to state that this man has no connection whatever with the Rivett-Carnacs whose name has been famous throughout Anglo-Indian history. His only connection with India is that he served as a gunner there, and during his few months' service created a record in the commission of military crimes.

Eventually he reached this country, where his stories of adventure in India and South America so impressed the editor of a certain newspaper that Carnac was given a free hand (financially) to run the story of three "Persian princes" he had found travelling incognito in London.

These princes were publicised in the paper, fêted, and photographed occupying Royal boxes at various London theatres, their picturesque robes and weight of jewels making them the sensation of the hour.

Not until the Persian Legation announced that no such princes existed was it revealed how "Bobby" Carnac had dug up three native seamen from dockland, rigged them out at a theatrical costumier's in the East End, and foisted them upon the paper as Persian princes.

Even this exposure did not end his activities, for, between several terms of imprisonment and one period in a lunatic asylum, he related such wondrous tales of his thrilling escapes from death in Mexico—where, he claimed, he was leading Generalissimo of the reigning President, and lover of the President's sister—that he was able to impose on influential people. One of his stories was that he had been incarcerated in a lunatic asylum over here because certain members of the Cabinet were afraid he might betray what he had learned about their traitorous activities during the First World War.

Lest it be thought that all masqueraders are of the male sex, it may be as well to tell the stories of some of the more spectacular of their feminine counterparts. Let us take the case of a fascinating adventuress whose attractions were as great as her intelligence.

We will call her Una, but I knew her under a number of aliases, ranging from that of a titled lady to that of a practising doctor, with the letters M.B.E., M.B., and B.Sc., London, after her assumed name.

Claiming to be the daughter of a general, on one occasion, and of a Fleet surgeon on another, she was in fact the illegitimate daughter of a woman who died in childbirth. Her father had provided her, however, with a sound education, and when Una was first launched into the world at the age of eighteen she met a young chemist whom she married in 1911.

Two children were born to them, and the husband obtained an appointment at Leeds. It was here that Una first took to crime. In the summer of 1919, it came to the husband's knowledge that his wife had cajoled various city people into parting with thousands of pounds, had cashed worthless cheques with trusting tradesmen, and had swindled a number of Army officers.

To one of the latter she told some tale about being a Ward

in Chancery, and persuaded him, on promise of future repayment, to advance her £3,185 for the purpose of starting a nursing home in the district.

The poor husband was compelled to go bankrupt, and Una went to Scarborough where she left a trail of worthless cheques behind her before she departed for London. There she tried to win back her husband; but the sincerity of her efforts may be judged from the fact that at the same time she went through a form of marriage with a Brigadier General. To him she represented herself as the widow of a naval surgeon, and claimed to be a fully-qualified doctor.

She obtained a position at a Dublin hospital by means of false credentials and bogus degrees, and after having been found out, came to London, where she attended students' classes at St. Mary's Hospital, Paddington, and afterwards at the Queen Charlotte Hospital.

After this she gave out that her father had been a Fleet surgeon who had died in action and had been granted a posthumous knighthood. As she was the only surviving child, she said, His Majesty had been pleased to confer the title on her.

So Una appeared for some months afterwards, in the West End of London and anywhere else her fancy might take her, as "Lady ——". And always there were impressionable and wealthy men ready to listen to her.

The next time I heard of Una she was charged with acting as *locum tenens* for a doctor in Maida Vale, attending operations and signing death certificates. The amount of the fine was £80 and 20 guineas costs, but Una preferred to go to prison for two months in default. That was early in February, 1925. In March of that year I saw her at the Old Bailey where she was charged with bigamy.

I well remember the words of the Common Serjeant at that time as he passed sentence of six months' imprisonment.

"I have nothing to do with the frauds you committed," he told her sternly. "I have to sentence you for bigamy. By your reckless extravagance and conduct, you made it impossible for your husband to live with you and you parted. You contrived by a mass of lies and by representing that you were a widow to contract a marriage with General ——. There are some cases where bigamy is not a serious thing with a woman, but I look upon this as a serious case.''

In October the same year Una had the distinction of being divorced by two men on the same day. Her legal husband secured a decree nisi, while the Brigadier General obtained an annulment. The papers were served on her in Holloway Gaol.

It is some years since I was present at a trial in which she figured, and I often wonder what she is doing now.

I could go on relating story after story of crooks of all types, spectacular and otherwise; the resourceful exploits of ''Bludger Bill'' Warren, the King of Confidence Tricksters, and the bogus Colonel Lawrence, whom I had no difficulty in exposing when he sought to sell the story of his disappearance and pretended death to the paper on which I was employed. You see, I had met Lawrence on more than one occasion, and I had seen this man sentenced for precisely the same imposture a year or two previously, and remembered him. Since then he has been sent down for another five years at Exeter on a similar charge.

There is not space enough in one volume to deal with every trial which has taken place at the Old Bailey, and for that reason I am deliberately omitting many of the most sensational dramas which have been played out within its walls, mainly those which have already been widely written about.

But there is one to which reference must be made, not because it was a *cause célèbre*, but because it is an example of the fallibility of human justice. It resulted in the quashing of a conviction for murder, the first appeal of its kind ever to be heard in the newly-constituted Court of Criminal Appeal.

This Court was set up in 1907. Before that date a convicted criminal could not appeal against his conviction or sentence. He had to rely on the intervention of the Home Secretary.

No. 1 Court in the Central Criminal Court today

Photo: Bedford Lemere

In 1911 a young labourer named Charles Ellsome murdered Rose Pender, a nineteen-years-old girl with whom he had been living. Neither of them was a very nice character, Rose being a prostitute, and Charles being content to live upon her earnings.

Eventually the girl left him, and Charles then went about muttering threats that he would "do her in". He also bought a long chef's knife, so that when, in the early hours of one morning, her dead body was found lying on the pavement with several stab wounds, suspicion turned upon Ellsome and he was arrested.

The most important witness against him was a man named Jack Fletcher who shared a room with two other prostitutes. This man described how, on the morning of the tragedy, Ellsome called, "Jack—Jack!" outside his bedroom window. When Fletcher opened the window, Ellsome told him he had "killed Rosie stone dead".

Fletcher made two statements to the police, but only one was put in evidence at the trial of Ellsome, and it was because of a confusion about these two statements that the learned judge, Mr Justice Avory, committed the error by which Ellsome escaped with his life.

Obviously Fletcher's evidence could not be accepted without corroboration. He did not show up too well in the witness-box, and under cross-examination defiantly told the court, "I thieve for my living and am proud of it."

Ellsome also gave evidence, denying that he had murdered the girl, and produced an alibi. But neither his alibi nor his evidence carried conviction.

The judge began his summing-up. Scrupulously fair as always, he emphasised the fact that Fletcher's evidence could not be accepted without corroboration, but pointed out that his evidence *was* corroborated by a statement he made immediately after the murder.

It so happened that this particular statement had not been

produced at the trial, and was therefore "not in evidence", as it is termed. It was a second statement which had been "put in".

The jury retired, and in due course returned their verdict of Guilty. I can still see the red-robed judge as he commented on the degraded life of the doomed man, before he uttered the grim words, "For the crime of which he has been convicted he must die."

Ellsome bore himself with stolid calm. I am sure that there was no more surprised man than he when, a few weeks later, his legal advisers having noted the flaw in summing-up, he heard Mr Justice Darling at the Court of Criminal Appeal set aside his conviction, and he was allowed to leave the court a free man.

It was the first capital case in which a conviction had been quashed. Charles was a very lucky man.

CHAPTER FIFTEEN

ECHO OF THE OSCAR WILDE CASE

A YEAR or two after the appeal of Charles Ellsome there occurred a trial which was an echo of one of the most sensational, dramatic, and tragic trials of the last century.

In the year 1895 Oscar Wilde was at the zenith of his literary prowess and social popularity. But in the April of that year, this great poet, author and master of paradox was stripped of his glamour and appeal when his action for criminal libel against the Marquess of Queensberry was dismissed. Wilde was revealed to public gaze as a sensualist, pervert, and practitioner of the Hellenic cult.

The Marquess was determined to expose Wilde because he believed that the latter had corrupted his son, Lord Alfred Douglas, and because he saw no other means of breaking their association except by exposing Wilde to the world.

To this end he handed in to Wilde's club an open postcard on which he had written, "Oscar Wilde posing as Sodomite."

It had the desired effect. Wilde brought an action for criminal libel, and there ensued that dramatic duel between the late Lord Carson, one of the most deadly cross-examiners at the Bar, and the egotistical, brilliant, but brittle Wilde. His epigrams availed him nothing against so dour a counsel as Carson, and Wilde's case collapsed, as did the poet himself.

Within three days Wilde was arrested and charged at the Old Sessions House with gross indecency with one Arthur Taylor, who stood beside him in the dock.

The Court was thronged to suffocation with friends of Wilde

and people in high society, who were avid to hear the unsavoury details of the evidence.

At the first trial the jury disagreed, and a month elapsed before Wilde and Taylor again appeared in the dock. Wilde was defended by the late Sir Edward Clarke, Q.C., who, in one of his greatest speeches, made so eloquent an appeal for his client that the Court rang with applause when finally he sat down.

His eloquence proved of no avail, however, for both Wilde and Taylor were sentenced to two years' imprisonment. Wilde went to the prison at Reading to serve his sentence, and to write, subsequently, one of his greatest poems, *The Ballad of Reading Gaol.*

On his release from prison Wilde went to live on the Continent. Even to the end he maintained his erotic ideas, painted his face and mouthed his epigrams. But he died almost in penury, a wizened old man of 44, in 1900.

I often wonder what those stylish friends of Wilde thought as they sat in that stuffy Court (in the *old* Sessions House) awaiting the return of the jury. Did they spare a thought for the poor devil below yearning yet dreading to know his fate? And what were Wilde's reactions to the grim surroundings, which, years before, Dickens had described as a "stone dungeon eight feet long by six wide with a bench under which were a common rug, a Bible and a Prayer Book, with an iron candlestick fixed into the wall".

The old Court, as we know, was dingy and ill-lit. And, although its dock was fairly roomy, the rest of the court was very cramped. There were no steps leading straight from the dock to the cells below as there are to-day. The prisoner had to step from the dock into the well of the Court, and then stoop down to pass through the little low door on the left, connecting the courtroom with Dead Man's Walk along which he passed to the dour old prison next door.

The proceedings which echoed Wilde's trial took place in

the new Old Bailey, but before I give the details of the case it might be as well to consider the changes which occurred during the intervening years.

To-day the gaol is gone. Dead Man's Walk still remains, or at least the site of it; for, when the new Old Bailey was built on the spot where Newgate Gaol stood, it was necessary to provide new foundations. Dead Man's Walk, with its historic flag-stones covering the graveyard of the hanged, suffered in the general disturbance.

The remains of the unhallowed dead were disinterred and taken to the City of London Cemetery where they were re-buried.

But the Walk is still there, running along the back of the present court in the same way that it ran along the prison wall of Newgate before its demolition. It is still known as Dead Man's Walk. For, if there should chance to be an overflow of water from one of the rooms backing on to it, the Works Department will be told, and when they ask where the trouble is will receive the reply, "About halfway along Dead Man's Walk", or wherever it happens to be.

There is nothing sinister about the appearance of this place to-day. Instead of the grimy, dank walls bearing the carved initials of the doomed, and instead of the heavy grey flag-stones upon which the hapless prisoner trod, there is a plain cemented walk, and the buildings on either side are walled with gleaming white tiles. Nor is there any iron grille overhead, as there was in the old walk, to make this promenade of death a more depressing place for all those who trod it.

Nor are the cells as gloomy and insanitary as they were before the year 1907, when the new Sessions House was opened. There is no suggestion of luxury about them, but they are not stuffy or insanitary. They possess a form and a table, both of which are screwed to the floor so that they cannot be used as weapons by any recalcitrant prisoner.

The walls are tiled about half-way up, and the rest of the

cell is distempered. Now and again a ribald prisoner will scribble a humorous rhyme upon the walls, and some of the more vainglorious, anxious to preserve their identity with the Old Bailey, will carve their initials deep into the walls. Among them have been some of the most notorious murderers of this present century.

Some of the verses which have been scrawled upon these walls have achieved a certain wit, even if they have not reached any great height of lyrical beauty or philosophy. It is a pity that no record has been kept. Other scrawls have expressed the writers' opinion of learned judges, and these, I may mention, would *not* be fit for publication.

There are ninety cells in the Old Bailey to-day; the women prisoners in a different corridor from the male prisoners. The cell in which it is usual to place those on trial for murder is not kept exclusively for this purpose. Other accused persons are placed in it when there is no occupant on the capital charge. Thus they can—if inclined to a perverse vanity—boast that they have been in the cell occupied by Crippen, Smith (the "Brides in the Bath" slayer), Bywaters, Ronald True, Seddon, Voisin, Heath and Thomas.

A contrast, this cell, to the dingy and gloomy place in old Newgate Gaol, referred to by Dickens. There is as great a contrast in the upper regions of the two Courts. I have already described the dark wooden staircase of the old Court, and the musty atmosphere of the courtrooms themselves. In comparison one can only say that the new building is a veritable "palace of justice", for its four storeys as viewed from old St Sepulchre's Churchyard present an imposing picture.

As one mounts the wide sweep of steps to enter the lower hall, it is difficult to recall that scores of unhappy malefactors met their doom on gallows erected outside the Debtors' Door of the prison on this very spot.

It is a handosme and majestic hall which one enters, extending almost the whole length of the building. In the centre is a lofty, marble-pillared place where the statues of four Kings of England stand in solemn majesty, Charles I and II, James I, and George IV.

Immediately in front of the entrance is the magnificent alabaster and marble staircase sweeping broadly upwards from the lower hall, and gracefully turning at a halfway landing to mount once more into the larger upper hall.

Before the blast from the 1941 bomb played havoc with this hall, it was a place of eloquent beauty. Immediately overhead was the great dome, on the panels of which were allegorical paintings by Professor Moira, illustrating Truth, Wisdom, Knowledge and Labour. There are also four figures (still intact, fortunately) supporting the dome and representing Justice, Mercy, Charity and Prudence, the work of Mr Pomeroy, A.R.A.

At the south end of the great hall is a painting by Professor Moira showing the looming outline of St Paul's Cathedral behind the figure of Justice, with several prominent statesmen and leaders of the Church kneeling in homage before her.

At the north end of the hall was another picture (destroyed, alas!), a beautiful pastoral scene painted by Sir William Richmond, R.A., called "The Golden Age", containing a group of nude figures. And I remember a very eminent counsel remarking to me one day as we passed through the hall on our way to Number One Court:

"You see those people in the picture, Bernard?" (pointing to the fully clothed figures in the Homage to Justice painting). "That's how they are when they come here. And that—" (turning round and pointing to the undraped figures of Sir William Richmond's "The Golden Age" at the other end of the hall)—"is how they are when we have done with them. Stripped of everything—honour, character, wealth and even life."

A facetious enough remark, but not without some element of truth, one may think.

The four courts leading from this hall are more spacious and business-like in construction than the old courts were. They are oak-panelled, and from each dock stone steps lead down directly into the cells below. There is ample room for counsel and the Press, nor are the jury so cramped for accommodation. The public no longer have to traverse the upper and lower halls to gain entrance to the public galleries (nor pay any fee for the privilege). There are private entrances for judges, counsel, and officials connected with the Courts.

All around the building on its various floors is a maze of private rooms for various purposes. The most ornate, in a dignified way, is the special room set aside for the Lord Mayor. It is a room of richly panelled oak and suitable furnishings. There is the Bar Mess, where counsel engaged in cases can obtain a meal. But there are no judicial "feasts" these days such as I have described elsewhere.

There is also the Judge's dining-room in which it is the privilege of the Lord Mayor and Sheriffs to entertain the Judges and other guests to lunch, a hospitality so well in keeping with City traditions.

There is no need, nowadays, for the posies of sweet herbs or rue to offset smell from the cells below, although that picturesque little ceremonial of the Judges and Commissioners carrying them into Court is still retained.

I recall a very old-world gesture by the late Mr. Justice Charles, the bachelor judge, after the acquittal of three men on charges of being habitual criminals. They had previously been found guilty of conspiring to forge and utter cheques.

Mr Justice Charles took up his bouquet from the Bench and looked across at the jury.

"I see there are two ladies on the jury," he remarked, "and I have only one bouquet. I think one of you ought to have it. I must not encourage gambling," he added with a twinkle in his kindly eyes, "but I suppose you must toss up for it."

With that he passed the posy across to the foreman of the jury who handed it to the older woman of the two, the younger having graciously assented to waive her claim.

It was this same judge who enlivened Number One Court on another occasion when he asked a witness if the young man in the dock was in a position to marry.

"Yes," replied the witness with confidence. "He is in a good job and could marry."

Mr Justice Charles shook his head, and in his deep voice remarked, "I'm in a good job, but no one ever wants to marry me."

The next morning he was inundated with offers of marriage from all over the country, but he is still a bachelor.

But we are anticipating our story.

Fourteen years after Oscar Wilde's death, on the very eve of the First World War, the late T. W. H. Crosland appeared at the Old Bailey, charged jointly with Lord Alfred Douglas with having conspired to bring a false charge against Robert Ross. The latter had been a great friend of Wilde during his life, and was Wilde's literary executor after his death. Lord Alfred Douglas had also been Wilde's friend, you will recall, and between Ross and him there existed a bitter literary feud, which came to a climax when Lord Alfred brought an action for libel against a man named Ransome because of certain aspersions made against him in a book entitled *A Critical Study*. The defence made use of letters and documents which had been handed to them by Ross, and Lord Alfred lost his case. He wrote a very scurrilous and threatening letter to Ross.

Not long afterwards a youth named Garratt went to Scotland Yard and declared he had been seduced by Ross. The case collapsed for lack of prosecution, and the action against Crosland and Lord Alfred (who were joint editors of *The Academy*) was then instituted.

Lord Alfred Douglas left the country, thus forfeiting his bail, but dear, rugged Crosland was there to answer the charges against him. As great a *littérateur* in his way as either Wilde or Lord Alfred Douglas, Crosland comported himself with the fiery humour which the crowd that thronged the court expected.

F. E. Smith (later Lord Birkenhead) opened for the prosecution. Mr Cecil Hayes appeared for Crosland.

The allegation was that Crosland and Lord Alfred had talked a youth named Garratt (then serving a term of imprisonment for importuning) into making a false statement concerning Ross. Ross, a smiling, well-dressed, dapper man, answered his leader's questions with a too-assured readiness. But he wilted under the cross-examination of Mr Hayes. The latter read a letter written by Ross's parents in which they referred to their son as "a disgrace to the family, a social outcast, and a son and brother unfit for society of any kind".

A flush spread over the face of the man in the witness-box, but there was still a note of truculence (or was it insolence?) in his voice as he said:

"My people objected to my association with Douglas."

"Not with Wilde?"

"No, Douglas."

The whole case was one of each side trying to discredit the other, and counsel on either side devoted themselves to this end. Mr Hayes continued by asking Ross about Wilde's *Portrait of Dorian Gray*, which the witness said was "a perfectly moral book".

Asked by the judge, Mr Justice Avory, if he thought there could be any such thing as an immoral book, Ross beamed with joy as he replied, "Yes . . . Lord Alfred Douglas's poems, for instance."

Crosland leaned over the dock in rage, and spluttered something unintelligible. In the witness-box he was more coherent and amusing. He did not deny the brilliance of Wilde's works but he considered them dangerous. In Wilde's preface to *Dorian Gray* is a sentence, "There is not a moral or an immoral book. Books are well or badly written." Commenting on this aphorism, Crosland said, "That is the stand-by of all people who write dirty books."

He declared that the boy Garratt had stated that he knew Ross, and that the statement he made was voluntary.

F. E. Smith was his own subtle self; and, after having gained an admission from Crosland that he regarded Lord Alfred Douglas as a suitable colleague, counsel read an extract from Lord Alfred's poem *Two Lovers.*

Then, with eyes fixed on Crosland, he demanded, "Have you any doubt that the reference contained in that verse is to unnatural affection?"

Crosland could only admit that it was. One could feel the sorrow in his voice as he made this answer, but a moment later he had recovered and was making brilliant sallies in response to questions.

Thus, when questioned about Ross, he replied, "I don't care if a man makes a hog of himself, but I do object to him making the world his sty"—a remark as witty as anything that ever fell from the lips of Wilde.

Again, when F. E. Smith remarked, after one of Crosland's comments, that the jury could take care of themselves, the witness responded dryly, "I have no doubt they can. I want them to take care of *me.*"

Even the stern face of Mr Justice Avory broke into a brief smile at this, while the jury simply roared with laughter, especially as Crossland continued, "I am here to fight with one of the finest intellects in England and I'm going to fight."

"Two thousand quids'-worth of Counsel against a poor man," was how he described the battle.

There was something refreshing about the attitude of Crosland to F. E. Smith. In no way awed, he spoke to the K.C. with an air of familiarity that endeared him to all.

"As a man gets older he will become riper," he said once, adding, "And as you grow older, Mr Smith, you will become riper."

It was certainly a day out for those of us privileged to listen, for in addition to the evidence, there was a "breeze" between Smith and the judge. Counsel made some utterly unwarranted remark about the jury drawing an inference that "in some parts of the case His Lordship has adopted views which are not those I had put before you".

It was a foolish thing to say before a judge so eminently fair and with such mastery of acidulated English, and in his summing-up, Mr Justice Avory dealt with the point with obliterating irony.

"It is certainly unnecessary," he said, "for counsel to remind you or to suggest that you are not to be influenced by any view that I might take of the facts. And it is unnecessary for me to remind you that you should not be influenced by any view that counsel for the prosecution took . . . You are not here to admire the advocacy of Mr Ross's learned counsel, and you are certainly not here to convict anybody merely because Mr Ross had the good fortune to have secured the services of one of the most eloquent and most eminent of the counsel at the English Bar. The question is whether the defendant knew that the charge against the prosecutor was false."

The judge then went on to state the real issues in the case, and commented on what he termed the "dangers" of the Criminal Evidence Act of 1898. Under this Act a prisoner is entitled to go into the witness-box and give evidence on oath in his own behalf.

Mr Justice Avory pointed out, "Before that Act no one ever lost sight of that grand principle of our criminal law that no man is liable to be convicted unless the prosecution has satisfied the jury beyond any reasonable doubt of his guilt . . . The moment the law was altered there was a danger that if a man went into the witness-box the jury might think it was for him to establish his innocence."

In this case the jury were only absent half an hour before returning a verdict of Not Guilty.

CHAPTER SIXTEEN

GOLIATHS OF CRIME

IT is a chastening reflection to consider how often financial Goliaths have fallen to the slings of the David of their own lust for wealth and power.

Many of those who have fallen have found their way into the dock at the Old Bailey, doubtless because the City surrounding the Court is the very hub of finance, with its Stock Exchange, its headquarters of great financial houses, and its inevitable lure for those with ambition.

Looking back, one sees, as though in procession, a number of remarkable wizards of finance who have ended in gaol *via* the dock at the Old Bailey—Jabez Balfour, Hooley, Bottomley, and Gerard Lee Bevan to mention a few at random. There were others, some of them fine men at heart, simply caught up in the mesh of their own gigantic operations and turning to dishonesty in the hope of gaining time to weather the financial storm.

This is no defence in law, however, no matter how extenuating the circumstances.

The story of Gerard Lee Bevan, a Jekyll and Hyde in the realms of fraudulent finance, has no parallel in the history of City crashes.

A Jekyll and Hyde I have termed him, and this is no loose description. As an undergraduate at Oxford, he was renowned for his piety and religious zeal. In London, too, he was looked upon as a man of impeccable honesty and trustworthy purpose. He gathered around him on his board of directors many of the highest in the land, men and women whose names were household words in high society and the world of finance.

He had a fabulous 16th century country mansion near

Hungerford, in Wiltshire, which was a treasure house of works of art. He came of a great and honoured banking family, was a genius in the City where he seemed to have the Midas touch, had a suite at the Carlton Hotel in which he entertained lavishly, and was gladly accepted in the highest social circles.

But when the crash came, he cravenly bolted to the Continent with a woman who was not his wife, grew a beard and dyed his hair to disguise himself, and feigned violent madness while fighting to resist arrest.

What a crash it was! There is no need to discuss in detail the sixteen counts charging him with publishing false reports and balance sheets of the City Equitable Fire Insurance Co. Ltd., except to say that Gerard Lee Bevan produced big dividends as if by magic. They rose from 88 per cent to 200 per cent in three years. The Company's £1 shares, originally priced at 4s, rose to £12 10s. When the crash came they were worthless, and desperate holders tried in vain to sell them. No one would accept them even as a gift.

But let us enter Number One Court at the Old Bailey, and watch this unimpressive-looking man in a blue lounge suit with black tie and horn-rimmed spectacles, who stood in the dock.

The seats immediately behind counsel, invariably set apart for distinguished visitors, were thronged with notabilities from the City and Society. The presiding judge was Mr Justice Avory, a judge with wide experience of cases bristling with financial obscurities. Sir Ernest Pollock, K.C., appeared for the Crown, with Sir Richard Muir, Mr H. M. Giveen, and Mr Vernon Gattie to assist him. For Bevan there was Mr H. Maddocks, K.C., Mr Travers Humphreys (now Mr Justice Humphreys), Mr J. M. Tucker (now Mr Justice Tucker) and Mr Ronald Powell, to-day one of the most respected Metropolitan Police Court magistrates. It was as formidable an array of counsel on either side as could be gathered together.

All those present waited to hear what possible explanation Bevan could give of his balance sheets and subsequent flight. In his opening speech for the defence Mr Maddocks had suggested that the fraudulent balance sheets signed by Bevan were a little "window-dressing".

Like a douche of cold water the judge in his summing-up commented that there were two kinds of window-dressing. He used the simile of a shop-keeper who put into his window attractive goods at attractive prices, and then, when a customer handed over his money said, "I am sorry, I have got your money but I cannot deliver the goods because they are covered by a bill or because I have only borrowed them.

"So with the insurance or any other company. If they put into their balance sheets as assets, things which they do not possess or hold any legal title to, and said, 'But this is only window-dressing', it was no answer even if it were true."

In this manner a complicated financial process was simplified before a jury, who for twelve days sat through a trial of a highly technical nature.

Nor was Bevan himself too happy in the witness-box, although he gave his answers readily, and with a certain amount of assurance. In one of his answers, he said that when any big investment matter was coming up, he and a Mr Barclay and a Mr Thomas always discussed it first before the committee meeting.

"Had you all three knowledge of financial matters?" asked counsel.

"We had been engaged in finance all our lives. Mr Grenside (another director) was a solicitor."

Mr Justice Avory: "Is that meant to imply that therefore he knew nothing about finance?"

Evidence was given showing how Bevan had "used" another director of the company, by signing an agreement that this man should, in addition to the salary he was already receiving, be given another £5,000 a year free of income tax. The company was also to grant him a loan of £110,000 which was to be repaid in ten yearly amounts of £11,200. He was also to be given four per cent commission on the annual under-writing profits of the company. There was another provision that if at the end of eleven years the commission credited to him did not amount to £110,000, he was to be considered free of debt, and if the company should be wound up before the loan and interest had been repaid, this fortunate man and the company were to be free of all liability, and the balance of the loan and interest was to be cancelled.

This amazing agreement was entered on the balance sheet as a good loan.

Bevan declared that he had signed this document without reading it, but evidence had already been called to show that before this agreement, entered into on March 4, 1921, this same man had been advanced several sums amounting to nearly £100,000 on cheques drawn on the company by Bevan. Only one amount of £15,000 was authorised by any resolution of the board, although Bevan told the auditors that all had been authorised.

It was also proved that on each occasion when amounts were paid into the bank of this "borrower", a cheque for a similar amount made payable to Bevan would be drawn on this man's account within the next day or so.

Examining Bevan about this £110,000 agreement, his counsel asked, "And you know now, that it was only necessary for the company to go to pieces to absolve Marsell from all liability under the agreement?"

Before Bevan could reply the judge interjected, "And only necessary for him to misbehave himself so that the company *had* to dismiss him to absolve him."

"I did not know what was in it at the time," insisted Bevan, and his voice rose in reply to the judge's next question as to whether he defended that clause in the agreement.

"Of course I don't," he said heatedly. "It is insanity."

The stern-visaged little judge leaned back in his seat.

"It may be something worse," was all he said, but there was a wealth of significance in that mild comment.

In cross-examination Bevan was pressed to explain why he fled the country.

He replied that he had gone away at the request of somebody but he refused to name that somebody.

"You had no misgiving as to your own conduct?"—— "None."

"And you were not afraid to meet any question put to you?" ——"Not in the least."

And so the examination went on, the prisoner alert, resourceful, his quick-thinking brain appreciating fully the portent of the questioning.

Dealing with Bevan's responsibility as chairman of the companies involved the Judge said, in his summing-up, "Unless he signed the minutes with his eyes shut, it is almost impossible to believe that he could have signed them without seeing what was in them . . ."

And then, later, "The final fact in this case was, that the defendant left the country, and, by artful disguises of himself, and various stratagems, succeeded in evading arrest until June. If he had given any explanation of his leaving the country consistent with his innocence, his counsel would have been entitled to say, 'You must discard that from your consideration.' But what is his explanation? 'I was asked to go,' said Bevan. His learned counsel said, 'I am not at liberty to tell you.' But Bevan himself was at liberty to tell you."

Throughout the four hours of summing-up the accused displayed little or no emotion. It was only when the jury came back and the foreman began to repeat the word Guilty time after time as each count in the indictment was enumerated, that he showed any anxiety.

The foreman of the jury seemed a very young man, and I am sure he must have felt the tension of those long-drawn-out

N

moments of question and answer, as he uttered the one damning word to each count.

I watched Bevan, watched his eyes turning back and forth from foreman of the jury to Clerk of Arraigns; from Clerk of Arraigns to foreman of jury. At last he knew his fate—all but the length of imprisonment he must serve.

He turned his eyes towards the judge, and his face looked drawn and lined. But there was yet another formality to be gone through. His lordship asked Sir Richard Muir whether there were any circumstances which counsel thought should be brought to his notice regarding Bevan, and a deep flush flooded the urbane countenance of the financier, as he heard the cold measured voice of counsel tell the court that Bevan had lived a life of great extravagance, continuing, "He left the country with a woman who was not his wife, and he was living with another woman not his wife when he was arrested."

Counsel went on to tell of "people of quite small means" who had parted with "the whole means of their livelihood" on the faith of the false prospectus issued by Bevan.

There came the climax to this trial, when Mr Justice Avory, after having commented on the damage done in destroying public confidence in the commercial integrity of the City, passed sentence of seven years' penal servitude upon Bevan.

Calm, composed, and to outward appearance unmoved, Bevan heard the words which made of him a convict. Then, smartly, he turned about and strode down the steps to serve his long term of imprisonment.

Released from prison in 1927, Bevan went to France where he married the beautiful Frenchwoman who had accompanied him on his flight from London. Together they went to Havana, where Bevan remained the head of a distilling firm until his death in April, 1936.

Just as Goliaths of finance have come crashing to the ground, so, from time to time, Goliaths of the underworld of crime have over-reached themselves and found their way by Black

Maria or special car into the prison yard of the Old Bailey, and thence into the dock.

Joseph (Cammi) Grizzard was one of these; the unchallenged King of Receivers, and the engineer of the greatest pearl robbery in criminal history. The loot was a pearl necklace worth £136,000.

Joseph Grizzard was the master-mind behind some of the biggest jewel coups in the annals of crime. But none was bigger than the theft of a necklace of 61 pearls, gathered together over many years, and matched with all the skill of Hatton Garden's greatest pearl specialist, the late Max Mayer.

Cammi had organised the theft by a ruse as simple as it was successful. One of his gang, named Silverman, made friends with the postman who used to deliver registered packages to Max Mayer at Hatton Garden. Silverman had one room on the top floor of a building, a door or two away from the Mayer premises.

Needless to say the packages were always sealed, but Cammi arranged that a duplicate of the seal should be obtained on a piece of wax concealed in the hand of Silverman, who had momentarily handled a package addressed to Mayer.

Meanwhile the pearl necklace had been sent to Mayer's agents in Paris for possible sale in France. But there was no sale, and the necklace, packed in its morocco case, wrapped in tissue paper, and then placed in a specially made wooden box, was finally wrapped in blue linen paper, addressed and posted to Mayer in London, bearing upon it the recognised seals of his firm.

One can imagine Mayer's shock when the precious package was opened at his office, and it was seen to contain nothing but a piece of screwed up newspaper, and eleven oblong pieces of sugar.

The police of France and England were called in, but it was the efforts of two amateur detectives, out for the reward of £10,000 which was offered, who were responsible for bringing the notorious Cammi, and his three confederates, Jimmy Lockett, Simon Silverman, and Leiser Gutwirth, into the dock at the Old Bailey.

Their capture was the result of a most amazing stroke of luck. Gutwirth happened to meet on the Continent a distant relative named Brandstatter, and foolishly mentioned that he was engaged in trying to sell the necklace. Brandstatter at once thought of the £10,000 offered for its recovery, and kept in touch with Gutwirth. Later, he came to England with a nearer relative named Quadratstein, who posed as a prospective buyer.

Co-operating with the police, Brandstatter and Quadratstein met the four men at the old British Museum Tube Station in Holborn, where a dozen of the Yard's most brilliant officers, including my friends George Cornish, Percy Cooper, Percy Worth (afterwards Chief Constable) and a few others, were lying in wait.

The crooks were on their way down in the lift with the two amateur detectives—one as the prospective buyer—while the Scotland Yard men raced down the emergency stairs. The gang had just reached the platform when the detectives pounced on them, "bracelets" at the ready, and it was only a matter of seconds before they were all on their way to Bow Street, there to take their first steps on the way to gaol.

The prisoners and their homes were at once thoroughly searched, but the pearls were not found. Then one morning, a man named Horn, on his way to work, saw a small parcel lying in the gutter. He picked it up and opened it. Inside was an ordinary match-box. He pushed open the drawer part. and saw what he thought were coloured marbles.

He put the box in his pocket, and went to have a drink at a nearby public-house—blessed days, they were open early at that time—where he showed his find to some friends. They were equally unimpressed. But Horn was an honest man, and took his box to the police station, where he was given a receipt for "imitation pearls".

The sequel is well known. The pearls found in the gutter had been flung there by the wife of one of the confederates. Grizzard was sent to penal servitude for seven years. Lockett received a similar sentence, and I am glad to say remained an honest man after his release in 1919. Silverman's sentence was for five years, Gutwirth's for eighteen months, and both men were recommended for deportation afterwards.

That was not the only time that Grizzard became acquainted with the inside of a prison. In 1889 he had been sentenced for stealing cigars, but fourteen years passed before he was next arrested on a receiving charge. On this occasion he was acquitted. In 1909 he was the brains behind a £100,000 pearl robbery, for which two men, "Grimmy the Jockey", and another man named Higgins, were tried and convicted at the Old Bailey. In this case the pearls—about a thousand in number—were never recovered.

This was the famous Café Monico robbery, in which a French jewel merchant was shadowed from France to England and his habits studied for weeks. Cammi never hurried on a job, and always laid his plans to the last detail. It was found that the merchant, named Goldschmidt, used to lunch at the Monico, where he would go to the lavatory and wash his hands, placing his case of jewels on the side of the basin while he did so.

On the day of the robbery, he was just reaching out for the soap when an arm flashed past him and snatched the bag. The thief made off through the door with Mr Goldschmidt in pursuit. Cammi had arranged that another confederate should step in the way of the pursuer as he reached the door, and then, as Goldschmidt got to the other narrow exit, another confederate should fall to his knees and thus once more "accidentally" obstruct him. Meanwhile, the thief had made his escape in the swirl of traffic outside. Everything went off as planned.

Cammi, although suspected, could not be implicated, but

Grimshaw and Higgins were caught and sentenced. A little later, Cammi was arrested for harbouring a man for whom he had become bail on a receiving charge, and he was sentenced to five months' imprisonment.

Ever ready to finance a likely proposition, with a vast bank account always available, Cammi continued as the instigator of all sorts of robberies and thefts, but again he fell foul of the police and was sentenced for conspiring to obtain jewellery from a firm for sale to wealthy princes in India. That, at least, was the plausible tale with which his fellow conspirator, an ex-major in the army, secured jewellery worth about £11,000.

Suspicion fastened on Grizzard, and he and another man—not the major—were arrested, Cammi receiving twelve months' imprisonment in October, 1922. As it happened, this turned out to be a sentence of death, for Cammi became so ill in prison that he was released by the authorities and died at his home in Dalston a few months later, in 1923.

Four years passed before the major was arrested at Liverpool and sentenced to six months for his part in that crime.

Let us turn for a moment now to one of the most ingenious and amazing insurance frauds ever perpetrated.

It was carried out by a soft-voiced and sweet-faced woman whose name I withhold because, as the learned judge commented, the fraud she had practised had been carried out in the interests of an unworthy son.

Certainly when she entered the dock she looked as unlike the typical adventuress as could possibly be imagined. The charge against her was that of conspiring with her son and others to defraud the Prudential Assurance Company of £2,881.

The case against Mrs B———, as we will call her, was that, having insured her life for nearly £5,000 in two offices, and having made her son the chief beneficiary under her will, she pretended to be drowned.

It was a cunningly-devised scheme. First, Mrs B——— wrote

to her daughter saying that she was going to bathe near Chaney Beach, Ilfracombe, where she was on holiday.

She went out from her hotel, and did not return. Her clothes were found later in a cave on the Beach, and it was thought she had been drowned while bathing. Nobody seemed to notice that there was no purse or handbag among the belongings left in the cave, and although a boat with grappling irons was sent out, no body was ever recovered.

That same night a woman entered the Girls' Friendly Society hotel at Exeter and explained that she had lost her luggage on the train, and that she wanted a job as cook. She gave the name of Trixie Finch, but it was later revealed that Trixie was Mrs B———.

That she had staged her "drowning" convincingly will be obvious from the fact that the President of the Probate Court had no hesitation, on the evidence supplied, of presuming her death, with the result that the Prudential Assurance Company paid out the money to the executor of the will.

Meanwhile the "dead" woman's son had obtained an advance on the strength of the will, and had bought a motor-car in which he embarked on a tour of Wales. Within a week or two he was killed in a car accident.

As the result of a provision in Mrs B———'s will, a certain charity made a claim on her estate, and until the action was heard, the executor placed the money in the safe keeping of the Court of Chancery.

Needless to say, the position of Mrs B——— became very difficult. She tried several ways of getting out of the trouble, but failed, and eventually went out to New Zealand. From there she wrote to her daughter-in-law, who was amazed to learn that the woman whom she believed to be dead was very much alive. This daughter-in-law had married again, and showed her husband the letter. He very properly informed the police, and a warrant was issued for the mother's arrest. She was brought back to face her trial at the Old Bailey.

It was revealed in court that she was the widow of a licensee, who had been left comfortably off, but whose son, being lazy and addicted to drink, had dissipated much of her money.

She was defended by Mr St John Hutchinson, and stated that following an accident at Ilfracombe she lost her memory and did not know where she was.

"Had you any idea at that time of getting any money from the insurance company?" asked counsel. "None whatever," replied the witness.

"Did your son know you were alive?"——"No one knew it."

"Had your disappearance anything to do with getting money?"——"No. It is the last thing I should have thought of. I never received one farthing from it."

Mr Cecil Whiteley rose to cross-examine and at once placed his finger on the weak spot of her story.

"Why did you live as a servant all these years if you were not frightened of being discovered?" he demanded.

"I did not want to be worried over my son," came the reply.

Counsel then produced a document which was handed to the prisoner. It was a proposal form to insure her life for a further sum of £10,000. "Is that your signature?" he asked.

"It looks like it," answered the woman, in faltering tones, "but I don't remember."

It was a damning document in the eyes of the jury who found Mrs B—— Guilty.

Judge Atherley Jones was in compassionate mood.

In passing sentence of six months in the second division he commented:

"You attempted to obtain by fraud large sums of money from an insurance company but not for your own benefit. You did it in what you conceived to be the interests of an unworthy son . . . You played the part of a loyal mother but broke the laws of the country in doing so."

Mrs B—— was immediately released as she had been in custody for six months—the term of her sentence.

CHAPTER SEVENTEEN

MEN WHO KILLED TWICE

ONE of the most amazing murderers it has ever been my lot to meet was Frederick Field, who twice stood in the dock at the Old Bailey on charges of murder.

Double murders—where a person kills two people at the same time—are not infrequent, but the murders of two people by the same person, with an intervening period of time between the two crimes, are fortunately rare. I say fortunately, because it must either mean that the murderer has been undiscovered, or, if he has been brought to trial, has been found Not Guilty by a jury of his fellow men, and been given his freedom only to commit another crime.

We have seen how Palmer, the Rugeley poisoner, and Neill Cream, the squinting murderer, committed several crimes before they were brought to justice; and George Smith, of "Brides in the Bath" ill-fame, also murdered three "wives" before he reached the scaffold.

The case of Field was more unusual, because he was arrested and brought to trial in each case *on his own confession* that he had committed murder. On the first occasion—in spite of his confession—he was found Not Guilty and discharged. On the second occasion, he was not so fortunate, as we shall see.

On a Friday morning in October, 1931, the dead body of Norah Upchurch was found lying in the passage-way of an empty shop in Shaftesbury Avenue.

It was discovered by Field, who worked for a firm of sign-board fixers, and his foreman. Field had been at the shop on the previous day to remove a To Let board, and said that a man in plus-fours had come to him, alleging that he had leased the shop and asked for the keys, which Field handed over to him.

A hue and cry for the "man in plus-fours" produced no result, and suspicion rested on Field, who was closely questioned by police and coroner—and, I may add, newspaper reporters.

He was a cool customer, was Field, and even went so far as to identify a man as the mysterious plus-fours wearer to whom he had handed the keys. But it was proved that this man had no connection with the crime.

Two years went by. The murder of Norah Upchurch had been forgotten by the public, and had joined the list of "unsolved murders".

Then, in July, 1933, a man walked into Kemsley House, the offices of the *Daily Sketch* as it was then, and told my friend the late Nelson Leaver, the news editor, that he wanted to confess to the murder of Norah Upchurch. He made a long and detailed statement describing how he had inveigled her into the shop, strangled her and then made off with her handbag which, he declared, he had planted in a ditch at Rose Hill, Sutton.

Scotland Yard was informed, and Field was arrested by my old friend Chief-Inspector George Cornish and eventually brought to trial.

On the face of it there seemed to be no hope for Field. All the circumstances emphasised his guilt: his own confession; the fact that he had possession of the keys at the material time; his explanation of how he handed them to the untraced man in plus-fours.

It was September before he stepped nimbly into the dock, a lithe and good-looking fellow, fair-haired, with rather piercing eyes. On the Bench sat the late Mr Justice Swift, rubicund, dignified, portly, and sometimes a little pompous, with a habit of tapping insistently on his table to interrupt counsel or witness when he had some point to make.

Mr Eustace Fulton, now Sir Eustace Fulton, led for the

Crown, and Field was ably defended by Mr Marston Garcia.

In the sepulchral tones which are a most impressive feature of his advocacy, Mr Fulton opened the case against Field. He described how the body was found, and read aloud the confession made by Field to the police. In the course of this statement, Field had said, "I lost my temper and gripped her round the throat . . . she seemed to faint away and fell back out of my hands on to the floor. She did not scream or speak. I knew that something was seriously wrong when she fell back, and lost control of myself, and cannot remember exactly what happened afterwards . . ."

Later in the statement he declared, "The reason I have come to the police to give myself up is because I am fed up. My outlook is bad, and through arrangements I have made my wife and child will be better off without me."

Witnesses were called for the prosecution, and it seemed to be a clear case. But I have attended too many murder trials, and witnessed too many last-minute surprises, to decide that a certain verdict is inevitable.

Field was put into the witness-box, and strode across the court with eager, confident stride. He repeated his story of the man in plus-fours, and then was asked with dramatic directness by his counsel, Mr Garcia:

"Did you see the girl Norah Upchurch at all that night?"——"No."

"Did you know her personally or had you ever seen her?"——"No."

"I put it to you plainly. Did you kill that girl?"——"I did not," came the emphatic and startling reply—startling because it was in such bold contradiction to his own signed statement and confession.

Counsel went on, "The finger of suspicion has been pointing at you since the inquest?"—"Yes."

There was a pause. Everybody was awaiting the next question, the answer to which would tell them why he had confessed to a murder which he now declared he had never committed. It came softly from lips of counsel, yet with impressive clarity.

"Why did you go and make that untrue statement?"——

"I had no chance of proving my innocence," came the ready reply, and there poured from his lips what he meant by those words.

"I wanted the whole thing cleared up properly. The whole thing was left in the air. People said, 'This man has done it', I could not turn round and say, 'I have been proved innocent.' I could not do anything or say anything.

"I wanted to be arrested and put on my trial, because by doing that I could have my innocence proved properly."

Of course this *could* have been true. An innocent man writhing under a false suspicion, his life tormented by the whispers he heard going around, *might* be goaded into taking some such action.

When Field gave this explanation, Mr Justice Swift remarked drily, "It is a peculiar way of proving your innocence to say you are guilty of the murder."

But Field as promptly replied, "It was the only way."

Nor could cross-examination by Mr Fulton shake the accused man, and at the conclusion of his evidence, and when he had returned to the dock, the judge leaned forward and in casual tones, not as if a life might literally hang upon his words, asked Mr Fulton, "Do you think it is possible to convict upon the evidence?"

Mr Fulton bent his head, looked over his glasses at the learned judge—a mannerism of his—and replied, "I do not think so, my Lord."

So Mr Justice Swift turned to the jury. He explained the position in law. There was no evidence against Field except his own statement. It was very obvious that he was a liar, but they could not find a man guilty of murder simply because he was a liar. He therefore directed them to find a verdict of Not Guilty against Field, who was immediately discharged.

Not long after this, Field joined the R.A.F. as an aircraftman.

Five years elapsed; and then, in April, 1936, the body of a middle-aged widow, Mrs Beatrice Sutton, was found lying on a bed in her flat at Clapham, with two pillows over her face. She had died of suffocation.

Once more a hue and cry was raised, and there seemed to be no clue to the identity of the murderer.

Meanwhile, Field had absented himself from his R.A.F. unit at Hendon, and was posted as a deserter. From time to time he called on a woman friend who tried to persuade him to give himself up and face the consequences.

"I am not going back," he declared defiantly, whereupon the woman told him she had finished with him.

Mrs Sutton was murdered on the night of April 4. That night Field called on his woman friend and told her she would read about "something" in the newspapers. He was looking so wild and desperate that the woman's mother, who happened to be present, made an excuse to leave, and went round to telephone the police. She told them where they could find Field the deserter, and they came along and collected him.

There was no inkling in her mind that Field had murdered Mrs Sutton; nor did the police imagine for a moment that the deserter whom they had in charge awaiting an escort from Hendon, was none other than the man "wanted" for that crime.

It was not until Field made another "confession" that they realised their good fortune. They took his statement down in full detail, read it over to Field, and he signed it without hesitation. He gave a detailed description of the bed, and of the murdered woman's position upon it. He gave other details of the room's furniture, very accurate details, it turned out. He described how he had pressed the woman's throat, and mentioned other things which showed that he had an intimate knowledge of the crime.

Once again he stood in the dock at the Old Bailey charged with murder. And once more—with singular lack of originality—he went back on his "confession", varying his story but slightly from the story he had told at his previous trial.

Mr Justice Charles was the judge on this occasion, and it must have been a trifle disturbing to Field to find that Mr Eustace Fulton again appeared for the prosecution. Mr Fulton—and the newspapermen in the Press Box of Number One Court—knew that Field had been charged with murder once before, and had been discharged. But the jury, of course, knew nothing of his previous appearance in that dock, or of his acquittal on the previous charge.

In that same sepulchral voice, Mr Fulton described the finding of the body, and again read aloud Field's confession.

"I did it," Field stated. "I was fed up with being short of money, so I thought I would get what dough I could and do myself in, but when it came to it I hadn't got the guts . . . I went to her place and done her in, and, as you might say, put myself on the spot . . . I just murdered her because I wanted to murder someone. I had not the guts to take my own life, and I knew by doing it I should lose my own life."

There were in addition those damning details of the death chamber, and his description of how Mrs Sutton came by her death.

Mr St John Hutchinson appeared for Field, and after the witnesses for the prosecution had given evidence, he put his client into the witness-box. Field looked a fine, soldierly figure as he stood there in his R.A.F. uniform. But it was an unsoldierlike story that he told the court.

On the run as a deserter, he said, he had for two or three nights slept in cupboards under the stairs of the block of flats in which Mrs. Sutton lived. On the night of the tragedy he was again about to crawl into one of these cupboards when he heard sounds of a quarrel, and then saw a man come out of a flat, leaving the door open.

"I thought I would go in and see what was wrong," he told the spellbound court with an airy glibness. "I saw the woman on the bed. She had a pillow over her face . . . For a moment I did not know what to do. I knew if I called the police they would only say what was I doing there.

"Then it occurred to me that if I were to take the blame for anything wrong in there I could accomplish what I had not the courage to do—that is, to commit suicide."

The reason he wanted to commit suicide was the quarrel with his woman friend, he declared, and he thought that if he took the blame for the murder, his life would be taken by the hangman. That was the reason for his confession, said Field, a confession which was false from the point where he said he committed the murder.

Mr Fulton rose to cross-examine. He looked over his glasses at Field, then took them off and twiddled them between his fingers. He then asked his first question.

"If you wanted to confess to a murder you had not committed what could have been more convincing than to have put your head out of the window and called the police?"

There was a momentary pause as Field thought out his reply. At length it came—rather haltingly, and certainly without conviction.

"At that time I had not definitely decided to confess to the murder," he said.

"Why did you describe pressing her throat in your statement?"——"I assumed it."

"And you explained it in a way the doctors say she was murdered?"——"It was a pure supposition."

The trial was as good as over!

It was a cruel murder, as was the murder of Norah Upchurch, both of them committed for the little money possessed by the unfortunate victims.

And the only defence was the same in both cases—that his confession was false.

There was no lack of evidence in addition to Field's own statements on this occasion, and the jury were absent only some twenty minutes before they brought in a verdict of Guilty. Field stood smartly to attention while sentence of death was passed, and only the sobs of his woman friend broke the tense silence of that dramatic moment. He died deservedly upon the gallows.

That was in the year 1936.

Ten years later, another thrill of horror swept through the country at the murder, within a fortnight and at places far apart, of two young women.

The first victim was Margery Gardner, who was found lying dead from suffocation in a room at a Notting Hill hotel.

It was not so much the manner of her death which caused the shock, as the nature of the violence which had been wreaked upon her before death.

She had been beaten with a woven thong, and there were signs of seventeen lashes upon her naked body. Her ankles had been tied together, and there were livid marks upon her wrists which showed that they also had been tightly tied, and released. Violence had also been done to the woman's face.

Enquiries showed that the dead woman had been in the company of Neville George Clevely Heath, crook, braggart, imposter and sadist. It was in the room which Heath had rented at the hotel that the body was found.

Heath had a deplorable history of affairs with women. He was known to have indulged in all manner of vicious and depraved practices, and to have inflicted flagellation upon those of his many women friends who were content to submit to his perversions.

When, therefore, the body of Margery Gardner was discovered and her association with Heath known, the police forces of the entire country were concentrated on a hunt for this man, who had suddenly vanished from the hotel and from all his usual haunts.

Mrs Gardner was murdered on June 20, 1946, and on June 23 Heath arrived at an hotel in Bournemouth where he signed the register in the name of Group Captain Rupert Brooke. It was in keeping with his grandiose character that he should assume the name of the poet-hero of the First World War.

The search for Heath went on without result. A fortnight went by, and then, on July 3, when the police search was at its very height, came news of another brutal crime, the murder of Doreen Marshall, a pretty ex-Wren who had dined with "Rupert Brooke" at his hotel in Bournemouth on the night of the tragedy.

Her dead body, terribly slashed and mutilated, was found in a shrubbery not far from the hotel.

According to the medical evidence there had been blows to the head, and injury to the left chest, *tying of the wrists*, abrasions of the body as though it had been dragged across the ground—probably unclothed—and strictures of the neck.

All these injuries had been inflicted before death.

There were other mutilations to parts of the dead girl's body; horribly sadistic mutilations which could only be mentioned in part at his subsequent trial. These had been inflicted *after* death, in an access of sexual mania.

"Brooke" was questioned, and related how he had seen his guest part of the way home on the night they dined together, leaving her to go on alone after they had reached the pier. He was unperturbed and calm, and gave a disarming story of his meeting with the dead girl.

But an astute young Detective Constable of the Hampshire Police named Souter, to whom Heath made his statement, was watching him closely, and noticed that "Brooke" bore a remarkable likeness to the photograph of Heath which had been circulated to all police stations by Scotland Yard.

He challenged "Brooke" with being Heath, but the latter laughingly denied it. Souter was fairly certain however, and kept him at the Police Station until officers from the Yard arrived, when Heath was arrested.

The scene shifts to the Old Bailey. On September 24, Heath stepped into the dock to be charged with the murder of Mrs Margery Gardner.

Nor was this the first time he had appeared on a criminal charge at the Old Bailey. In July, 1938, he was sentenced to three years in Borstal for housebreaking and stealing jewellery and for obtaining clothing by fraud. Ten other cases were taken into consideration. He had posed as Lord Dudley and had defrauded people all over the country.

But now he faced a capital charge. And I would point out that he was *not* charged with the murder of Doreen Marshall, although evidence in that crime was given in court to show "system", as it is called in legal phraseology—in other words, that he had followed a systematic course of conduct.

Apart from a pair of sinisterly expressionless eyes, Heath was a good-looking young man. And certainly from the brisk manner with which he wrote copious notes to be handed down to his solicitor, and his general demeanour of being the chief character in this drama, there was little suggestion of the insanity which was raised as a defence on his behalf.

The court was packed, and crowds lined up outside the public gallery trying to gain entrance to the court. Heath was obviously pleased, as he gazed round from time to time, or lifted his eyes to the gallery.

Singularly enough, it was his own counsel, Mr J. D. Casswell (who has been successful in more than one murder case), who exposed Heath to the court as the crook and imposter that he was, and who showed that throughout his career in the R.A.F. Heath had given continual trouble, having been dismissed the service on three occasions.

It is unusual for the past record of a prisoner to be revealed to the jury before they return their verdict: and in this case it was only done to support the defence of partial insanity which had been raised, and to show Heath as an irresponsible and far from normal person.

Needless to say Heath was not put into the witness-box. Instead, Dr William Hubert, the famous psychiatrist, was called, and, giving the results of his examination of Heath after arrest, stated that in his opinion Heath was "not an ordinary sexual pervert, but he is suffering from moral insanity and at times is quite unaware that what he is doing is wrong".

"In your view is he certifiable as morally insane?" asked counsel.

"Yes," was the reply, the doctor adding, "I think he appreciated what he was doing and appreciated the consequences, but did not appreciate that what he was doing was wrong."

Mr Anthony Hawke, chief counsel for the Treasury, rose to cross-examine. He has much the voice and mannerism of his famous father, the late Mr Justice Hawke, and there was the same penetrating subtlety in his questions.

"I take it that at the time he murdered Mrs Gardner he knew he was doing something wrong?" he asked. "No," came the reply.

"Would he know what he was doing?"——"Yes."

"He knew he had bound and tied a young woman lying on a bed?"——"Yes."

"He knew he had either gagged or suffocated her by keeping her head pressed down?"——"Yes."

"He knew when he inflicted 17 lashes on her with a thong that he was inflicting 17 lashes with a thong?"——"Yes."

"And did he not know that they were wrong?"——"He knew the consequences."

"I did not ask that."—"He did not consider it wrong."

It was a great battle between expert witness and as expert a counsel.

Dr Hugh Grierson, Medical Officer at Brixton Prison, with a vast experience of mental cases among prisoners, was called to give evidence. After he had given a summary of his study of

Heath while the latter was in his charge, he stated that there was no evidence that the accused man suffered from any mental disease at the time of the occurrences.

This was also the view taken by the jury, for they found Heath Guilty, and he was sentenced to death.

All through the summing-up by Mr Justice Morris, Heath sat unperturbed, and it was not till the clerk of the court asked him whether he had anything to say that he displayed the least sign of emotion. There was a momentary twitching of his face as he uttered the one and only word he had uttered throughout his trial with the exception of the two words Not Guilty at the very beginning. They had been uttered almost with bravado. Now his voice seemed to be muffled as he replied to the clerk, "Nothing."

He stood to attention as sentence of death was passed and then, with one hand thrust into his trousers pocket, he turned and strode towards the steps leading to the cell below.

Thus perished two airmen on the scaffold, each guilty of the brutal slaying of two people.

Why did they do it, these two young men?

The murder of Norah Upchurch was a sordid crime of combined lust and robbery. Field was on the run, and desperate for money when he smothered Mrs Sutton. The murder of Mrs Gardner was in a different category altogether. I am convinced that when Heath took her to that Notting Hill Gate hotel, he had no intention of murdering his companion. I believe that they both repaired there for the sole purpose of indulging in an orgy of flagellation, and that Heath—perhaps to stifle the cries of his partner in perversion—gagged and unintentionally choked her. Finding her dead, he lost his head and ran away.

Then—far from insane—having committed one murder and knowing that sooner or later he would be run to earth, he cunningly determined to commit the second murder, to bolster up a plea of insanity so that his worthless life might be spared when he was brought to trial for the double crime. That too was the reason for the viciousness of the after-death mutilations upon his second victim.

The luckiest man who ever escaped the gallows, is how I would describe Donald George Thomas, a cheap and nasty crook who added wife-stealing to his other unpleasant habits.

We need not go into elaborate details of his crime, as it is of comparatively recent date. It will be remembered that Thomas shot a plain-clothes policeman and that in evidence it was stated he carried a loaded Lüger pistol wherever he went, and slept with it under his pillow "as a hobby".

One night, Thomas was stopped by a diligent and astute policeman, P.C. Nat Edgar, who questioned him about a number of burglaries in the district. While Edgar was trying to check the facts Thomas shot him dead.

When arrested in his bedroom, Thomas made a snatch at the Lüger which was under his pillow, but a police officer got there first.

Towards the end of April, 1948, George Thomas was brought before Mr Justice Hilbery to answer the charge of wilful murder. But in the meantime much had happened. The Criminal Justice Bill, containing a clause to suspend the death penalty for five years, had been passed by a free vote of the House of Commons, and was on its way to the House of Lords when Thomas stepped into the dock of Number One Court.

Once again history was to be made in the Old Bailey, and the court was filled when, after a patient hearing, the jury came back with their verdict of Guilty against Thomas.

I could just see a glimmer of a smile on the face of the murderer as he heard the hitherto fatal word Guilty fall from the lips of the foreman of the jury.

He knew well, as indeed we all knew, that even though he had been found guilty of as cold-blooded a murder as was ever committed, he would not suffer death upon the gallows.

Perhaps he was as curious as the rest of us to hear in what form sentence would be passed.

We had not long to wait, and to me, who so many times had heard the solemn words of the death sentence uttered in that court, it came as something of an anti-climax when the tradition of centuries was swept aside, and in easy, almost conversational tones, the judge said:

"The sentence of the court upon you is the sentence prescribed by the law, namely that you suffer death by hanging."

The judge wore no black cap—that was left lying on the desk in front of him, together with his white gloves. There was no formal ringing cry of the usher calling upon those present to remain silent while the sentence of death was passed. No Sheriff's vicar standing solemnly behind the judge to utter his final "Amen" as the last words of the death sentence were spoken.

In due course the sentence was commuted to one of imprisonment for life, which means that if he is of good behaviour in prison, and earns full remission, Thomas will be free at the latest in 1963, in which year he will still be only thirty-seven years of age.

A few others were sentenced under the new Act after Thomas, and the form of words varied slightly according to the judge presiding at the trial. All the prisoners were reprieved and sentenced to life imprisonment.

But so great became the spate of crimes of violence and murder, so loud were the protests of the public, reflected in letters to the Press and questions in Parliament, that in June —just two months after the suspension of the death penalty had come into operation—the clause in the Criminal Justice Bill which had brought about this reform was deleted, and Capital Punishment was restored.

Since then, the Old Bailey has more than once echoed to the solemn words of the death sentence.

Within quite recent times, Number One Court has written

yet another chapter in the story of justice. In March, 1949, Leonard Jack Thomas was charged with wounding with *intent to murder* his wife. In May he appeared in the dock at the Old Bailey where he was sent to prison for seven years, after it had been revealed that his wife was lying paralysed in hospital as the result of eleven vicious stab wounds.

A month later the wife died from her injuries, and Thomas was charged with her murder.

There is a legal axiom that no prisoner can twice be punished for the same crime, and when Thomas entered the dock at the Old Bailey for the second time, charged with murder, his counsel, Mr R. T. Paget, K.C., submitted that the accused man had already stood trial on what amounted to a charge of *attempted* murder, had been convicted and was serving a sentence for his crime. Counsel, therefore, on the grounds that Thomas was twice being put in peril of being convicted for attempted murder, entered a plea on his behalf of *autrefois convict* which means "already convicted on another occasion".

This is a very ancient plea, based on a law made during Plantagenet times (1154-1399), and it was on this alleged violation of a 600-year law that Mr Paget built the defence.

On July 13th an Old Bailey jury decided that Thomas *could* be tried for murder after being sentenced for a lesser offence. They were promptly resworn and on July 15th they found him guilty of wilful murder, but added a strong recommendation to mercy.

Sentence of death was passed with all the revived ceremonial of the black cap and the chaplain's "Amen".

It was the first case of its kind in the history of the Criminal Law of this country, and it is perhaps fitting that it should have taken place in the Old Bailey.

But the end was not yet. The execution of Thomas was provisionally fixed for August 3rd. Several days before that date an appeal was entered on his behalf, and on August 29th the condemned man appeared in the wide oak-panelled

Court of Criminal Appeal to hear his counsel make a final fight for his life.

Again Mr Paget emphasised his point that Thomas could have been convicted of *intent* to murder, and should not have been put in peril a second time, which was contrary to law.

Three learned judges sat to hear the appeal: Mr Justice Humphreys, our oldest and most experienced judge in criminal law, Mr Justice Hilbery, and Mr Justice Croom-Johnson.

They listened to counsel unfolding his legal arguments, and then Mr Justice Hilbery broke in . . . "What you say is that wounding with intent (the charge on which Thomas had been convicted in the first instance) is attempted murder?"

"I do," replied counsel.

"What is the mistake in law which you say the judge made at the trial?"

"The finding that Thomas had not been put in peril twice. I am saying he could have been convicted a second time for attempted murder."

Without calling upon counsel for the Crown to reply, the three judges decided that there had been no violation of that cherished principle of English law which has come down to us through the centuries, and that the sentence of death must stand.

Later, Mr Chuter Ede, the Home Secretary, thought fit to give expression to the jury's recommendation to mercy, and the death sentence was commuted to one of life imprisonment.

CHAPTER EIGHTEEN

THE OLD BAILEY OF THE FUTURE

I HAVE come to the end of my story of the Old Bailey so far as it can be told at present.

We have travelled far in time and have seen many changes. We have watched the evolution of justice in our land as meted out at this court throughout the centuries, and have witnessed the ever-growing humanity of our laws and their administration.

We have seen this historic Court survive the Great Fire of London, and its attempted destruction by the Gordon Rioters. And we have, in more recent years, proudly surveyed the new Old Bailey carrying on "Business as Usual" after one of Hitler's bombs had scored a direct hit on the Court.

We have not always had occasion to regard the Old Bailey with pride, nor the counsel who practised there, nor the Judges who presided at its trials. It was many years before the fervour with which our ancestors used to pray for "all prisoners and captives" became translated into practical measures for the more godly administration of justice and the betterment of prisoners.

To-day, however, we *are* entitled to be proud of the Old Bailey with its centuries of tradition, of which no other criminal court in the world can boast; of its picturesque ceremonials, and, above all, of the quality of justice assured to all who enter its walls.

What of its future?

At the moment of writing a City of London Corporation surveyor is engaged in drawing up plans to restore the blitzed Court. He stands at his drawing-board in a spacious room on the ground floor, the windows of which look down on Dead

Man's Walk. The plans have already been passed by the Corporation, and the reconstruction will cost some £200,000.

There will be six permanent Courts in place of the four now in existence. It is inevitable that with increasing population in the Greater London area, there should be an increase in the number of trials taking place at the Old Bailey. The Corporation of the City of London is emphatic that only the best and finest is worthy of the citizens of London, and is anxious that the repairs of the bomb damage shall afford opportunity to add to the amenities of the Central Criminal Court.

To outward appearance there will be no change, but inside there will be a playroom for the children of witnesses compelled to attend the Court. A matron will be in attendance, and toys will be provided for the entertainment of the children.

There will also be a licensed snack bar and restaurant where refreshments can be obtained. There will be separate accommodation for witnesses, police and jury, so that the latter shall be protected from any possibility of "tampering", or attempted influence.

Solicitors and counsel will be accommodated apart, that there may be no question of touting, and everything that can be humanly devised in the reconstruction of the building will be done to ensure that the quality of justice shall remain at the high standard it has already attained at the Old Bailey.

Yes, the City Corporation have every right to be proud of their Old Bailey. Legal luminaries from all over the world count it a privilege to sit on the bench beside learned Judge or Commissioner to see how justice is administered in our land. And they return to their own countries, good and powerful ambassadors on our behalf, to tell the story of the thousand years of tradition which lie behind this modern monument to our system of law and justice.

INDEX